MISSING FATHER

*A Daughter's Search for Love, Self-Acceptance,
and a Parent Lost in the World of Mental Illness*

MISSING FATHER

A Daughter's Search for Love, Self-Acceptance,
and a Parent Lost in the World of Mental Illness

Shauna L. Smith

Compassion Press

Do Not Stand at My Grave And Weep
— Mary Elizabeth Frye

The Land of Dreams
— William Blake

Photograph from the author's collection.

Library of Congress Cataloging in Publication Data is available

ISBN 978-0-9965457-0-9

Smith, Shauna L.
Missing Father

As this is memoir, my memories, on the elusive spectrum of reality and imagination, fact and fabrication, are my responsibility alone. With the exception of a few family members and friends, names and places have been changed and descriptions altered.

Published by Compassion Press, Ca., 2017

Printed in the USA

Cover design by Stefan Danielski

Father, O Father! what do we here,
In this land of unbelief and fear?
The Land of Dreams is better far
Above the light of the Morning Star.

— William Blake

Blessed are the cracked, for they shall let in the light.

— Groucho Marx

CONTENTS

PART ONE

BROKEN

The World Wasn't Made For People Like Him

THE BRASS RING on the merry-go-round, Coney Island boardwalk, circa 1948: I am with my Father, stepping up to the painted horse, the original paint, not yet dried up, flaked, or diminished by time, the horse held down by a pole hammered down its back with only a slow movement to the rhythm of a repetitious, uplifting melody, up and down, up and down, the motions reflecting my Father's moods, his slow, jarring decline as the years and his life took away his veneer and the substance and music of his being.

Mother was there too, taking the pictures; probably it was she who told my Father to lift me onto the stilled horse and bend down beside me. We are leaning in, a precarious balance between us, for a photograph moment before the music restarts and the merry-go-round resumes its circular up-and-down dance. My Father and I are smiling for the camera. Say cheese. Cheese. Snap.

One of the times my Father was high, he bought a blown-glass merry-go-round that I wish I still had to show my children. I seem to remember the delicate horses having tints of pinks and blues, yellows and greens. I don't know what happened to any of the treasures he bought on impulse—wallets and purses, decorative dish towels, perfume bottles, belts and scarves, a broach of a woman in a rose color, silver pins, one a spoon and one a fork, socks, smoked oysters and other exotic foods, and once a live baby duck that died in our apartment after a few hours.

When I read *The Glass Menagerie* in high school, I could see the small figurines as if they were in front of me, in my Father's hands. And I couldn't stop the sadness: Laura, the glass horses and unicorn, and my Father, all unable to find a place on earth where they could be safe. Once broken, impossible to repair.

Robert is the one who rides next to Kira and Chanti on the merry-go-round near our home.

He stands tall and proud of them as they hold onto the reins like the myriad other small children who patiently waited in line for their turns to brave the carousel dance. And I snap the photos as the music brings me back in time to a kaleidoscope of memories and forward to a future I hope will be less volatile for us and our children.

I DON'T REMEMBER very much before I was five, or everything seems inconsequential before then, or perhaps is repressed. Until one day and night, when it began in full force.

I was sitting on the maroon couch in the living room of our three-room apartment, watching the impossible. My Father and Mother were screaming at each other in turn, like in the *Punch and Judy* series on television, their faces distorted and full of hate. I don't know what the words were, just that they faced each other in rage, apparently unaware of anything but their fury, not at all aware of my five-year-old presence sitting stunned and silent on the old velvet maroon couch. All of a sudden my stomach felt exceedingly heavy in my body and as if things were spinning inside. I didn't want to vomit. I tried hard to swallow back the bitterness, and succeeded for a while. My eyes started tearing, however, from the anxiety and the strain, and finally, uncontrollably, I threw up all over myself and my jumpsuit, ugly colors all over the jumpsuit, the couch, and the bare wooden floor.

Mother strode over to me in the midst of her fury at my Father and smacked me across the face, engulfing me into her frustration and rage. I ran, alone, into the bathroom to take off my clothing and clean myself up while they renewed their fight. I heard something being thrown as I started to return and instinctively went over to Mother to protect her from whatever had happened. She, however, pushed me aside, sat down on the chair, and wept. I felt at that moment the most intense hatred for her that I could imagine and I know I have kept this toward her to this time, together with a beginning knowledge that she would never be able to surmount her own problems enough to afford time for me, certainly not at the times when we were both under pressure. Mother was, unfortunately, under stress a great deal of the time, and I soon learned not to count on her for comfort, although always I secretly hoped she would be able to give it to me gently, lovingly, of her own accord.

At any rate, I was stunned at her contempt of my sympathy as I understood it, and went in to see my Father, now in the bedroom. He was sitting on the bed with his hands on his face, and when he saw me he said the words: "She hit me in the ear. She hit me with her shoe in my ear." I can hear the words now, pounding in my head. We looked at each other in a bond against her that came of rejection by her. I had not understood what the words meant – how could Mother, who was shorter than my Father, kick his ear?—but I understood his distress and despair. Only years later was I able to puzzle together that she took off her shoe and hit him with it. The bizarre image of Mother kicking my Father in the ear haunted me through countless nightmares.

I sat by my Father and he put his arm around me and we stayed there for a long while in silence, comforting each other. I felt so close to him then, as if I would never leave his side. He did not yell at me for throwing up or for being around or wanting to be with him, even though he, too, was under incredible pressures, even though he, too, was being choked by broken dreams.

I dreamed that night in yellows and blues, a dream that recurred every few nights for at least a year. I was walking on the yellow land, alone and just being, when I heard sounds and, turning, saw all variety of wild animals, lions, tigers, and a rhinoceros coming at me ferociously and pitilessly. Terrified, I began to run and saw water so I sped on the earth till I fell into the light blue liquid and began to swim desperately for survival. Then I saw them – the crocodiles and alligators, coming up for air and heading for food among the rocks and growths. I tried to turn back but the animals were there on the shore and I began to scream, finally waking up in a deep sweat, shaking and grateful to be alive, until I would remember that the days were not that much unlike the nights.

I WOULD SIT at the old typewriter we had and press the keys to write small letters of caring to bring with me to the hospital. I couldn't go inside in those days, being too young, and, though I usually stayed with my grandparents, sometimes I was allowed to go with Mother and wait on the hospital grounds to see him, either from the window, screened in by wire, or downstairs for the half-hour of visiting time. Depending on his mood, my Father was either very witty, sometimes devastatingly so, hostile, or deeply depressed. When he was high he would go over to people and share with them the news that he felt wonderful; in fact, he would say, "I haven't had so much fun since my wife fell down the stairs." I didn't understand the words very well or the meaning of his ecstatic moods covering his feelings, but I did get caught up in his high spirits and engaging energy and felt happy being with him. It was incredible. He would sleep only two or three hours a night then and be rested and vital the next day. I always felt a tiny part of me reserved from him, though, during those times because of a distance I could not place, an odor that was about him as he ignored self-care, and the peculiar glaze in his silver-blue eyes.

I would talk to people on the grounds, on benches, or walking with their heads down, while I waited to see if my Father would be allowed to go out with Mother. They would say, "Hey, little girl, what's your name?" or "Do you have any money, little girl?" and I would sometimes talk with them or listen to their stories. Some people I saw consistently through the years, and I identified with them more than most people I met outside who I never felt I quite belonged with. Here were people who in their way had nothing to hide, nothing to pretend about, and I often liked being with them.

Though when I got older I feared greatly that I would naturally find my place there and, terrified, refused to acknowledge my kinship. One enormously fat man in a wrinkled white shirt would always be there swinging on the swing, his eyes vacant, drooling at the mouth, while his slovenly mother, hardly a visitor, pushed the swing, humming to herself. She would occasionally speak to him as if he were a child, telling him to hold on tight or button his sweater, but he never seemed to hear her from his half-hold on the world, and she would place his hands on the ropes, or close his sweater for him.

When my Father was high, he would wave to me from the third or fourth floor porch behind the wires and call down to me, and I would wave back. Once, when he was very high, he started pretending he was a monkey eating a banana and climbed up the fencing that was screened straight up to the next floor. I didn't think he was very funny then, because there were several other visitors there and they seemed appalled that he was climbing up the screening, shouting, "Look at me—see I'm a monkey in a cage, look at me everybody!"

I didn't let on that I didn't think he was funny, though, and when they let him come down he smiled at me sheepishly and picked me up gently in his arms, swinging me high around and around the world. It was easy then to stifle the hot shame. Besides, he had lots of friends at the hospital who liked him, and he would introduce me to them in such a wonderful way, as if I were an adult.

"Tom, this is my kid—put it there—Tom used to be an artist, and he's got—do you believe—a PhD!" He would put his hand to the side of his face in a gesture of wonder mixed with incredulity—"A lot of good that does him now, huh? Degrees don't do you much good in a nuthouse."

Then he would take me with him to another inmate, starting much the same kind of introduction.

One of his biggest laughs was to go over to someone who was depressed, put an arm around them and say, "You look wonderful today, sweetie, just wonderful," and at the first glimpse of hope from the sad face, add, "Who's your embalmer?" and usually the glimmer would disappear.

I really don't think he did this to be mean or was even aware of the person's pain. When my Father was "normal" he never did anything cruel, and perhaps this is part of the problem. I think he had so much pent-up feeling, so much anger and frustration, that it would all come tumbling out of his mouth unintentionally, covered up by exaggerated humor and boisterousness, and whoever was around became the hapless victim. Except for me, as far as I can remember. Except for me.

Mother generally took these times quite well while she was there, though she would be anxious and abrupt with me when we left. She would always get dressed up and be very clean and made-up when we went to the hospital to make sure she looked different from the patients, something that so many visitors never seemed to attempt to do. She spoke to people there but not "overly" much and was usually liked by the visitors, patients, and staff. They would tell my Father frequently what a wonderful wife he had and how lucky he was. But I had other information, and I knew better. Though I could not speak, I swear I always knew.

LOOKING AT THE date—10/2—I think of my Father always answering the question "What time is it?" with "Ten to" and when asked "Ten to what?" responding, "Your own business." Did he hear that from Milton Berle or Sid Caeser or his hero, Groucho Marx? Some were his own jokes, personal, clever, and to the point, but most I suppose were derivative—no: copied. I don't like to think that a lot of his humor wasn't his, that some belonged to studio writers and some to his symptomatology, for he had special qualities which I felt left no room for pretense or phoniness. Yet much was untrue and fragments of what could have been.

Try to clear my head, to think of things in steps instead of the entirety in images and flashes. Some one incident to hang on to, latch on to. Mother, telling me about the chief psychiatrist at Brooklyn State Hospital in 1948, a wonderful man who explained that the cause of mood swings was unrelated to her, and that electric shock was the treatment of choice. Mother had her hair done softly around her face then, her dresses were mid-calf and flowing, and she did not ever question authority.

The fact that my Father had been living with Mother and her parents, not working, with a child and a senseless life in his early thirties did not enter into the diagnosis that was made. Mother's higher educational status, a degree from college at a time when this was uncommon, and his education only through seventh grade, the bickering and criticism of her parents directed mainly at my Father, were not considered in the diagnosis. His parents' early deaths, not considered. Only the symptoms were discussed, only Mother's leaden feeling of guilt, not his, only the easy way out of an embarrassing situation: electric shock. Shock treatments in the days when they were agony to have, when people screamed having them as others waited in line in the filthy halls for their turn, shock treatments administered to my Father, once and again, and once more, and on and on for seventeen times in a month's period, till the glazed, manic look filled with vitality and passion and rage and humor was stricken from his face and he was left quiet, acquiescent, and beaten.

Who knows what was the cause? Surely in part a marriage of two unsuited people with basic weaknesses in both, each wanting what they could not give. One of the most damaging clues in letters I found in Mother's apartment years later, letters written when they were engaged, written with barely a fraction of knowledge of each other or of themselves. Two lonely people needing so much they never heard what the other was saying in their long-netted words.

One from Mother:

Dear Sam,

I am most happy that the frequency of your letters is increasing. However, the contents of your last letter have me a little worried. Are you as cold as your letter makes me feel? We have below zero temperature here too, but I don't find it so bad when I go out. My dad goes out every day. He's outdoors a lot. He says it's pretty bad—but not so awful. Do you find that approximately the same temperature is much worse in Mass. than in NY? And do you think it is due to the difference in climactic conditions?

Perhaps you ought to dress warmer? How about buying some woolen socks and gloves; also a pair of high boots to keep the snow away from your feet. It would be a good idea also to get a cap with earflaps to keep from getting head colds. And I do hope you're wearing a warm scarf!

You are now starting your third week of work, are you not? It is too bad Kozy had to quit so soon. Couldn't he stick it out a little longer so that he could cover his expenses?

By the way, how did he go home—by train? What arrangements did you boys make with him about the car?

By the way, what did you mean by that crack about my keeping a copy of my questionnaires so that all you have to do is answer yes or no? Are you too tired or lazy or is it too much trouble to answer me? Or is it too cold where you are? If it's too cold (I refuse to believe the first reason) you should do something about moving into warmer quarters. You are not living in a cold place, are you? If you are—I wish I had you here on my knee to administer a thorough spanking. Move out of there IMMEDIATELY. Get a WARM place. And be sure to keep your hands, <u>feet</u>, neck and ears warm when you are outdoors. Then you won't have to worry about being cold. And don't be afraid to spend money on these things. They are "necessities."

Of course, it would be best if you could get the truck-driver's job so that you would be out of the snow. Have the chances of your getting it increased? How are the rest of the boys standing it? Don't let anyone discourage you & make you lose the one chance you have of at least getting into a union. Did Irving ever come down? If he is having trouble keeping his hands warm, tell him to wear a glove on his left hand and just cut off the tips of the fingers from the glove so he can hold the nails.

As for myself—I am quite happy in my new work. At the end of my second day, I can safely say that although my supervisor is not a peach and is rather a fussy thing she is 50% (even 75%) improvement over Miss Roseman. The work I am doing is much easier so far. I am not rushed. I actually get plenty of rest in between. The people I work with are very....

It is hard to go on. Clear within the lines, the comparisons, criticisms and suffocation. All interpreted by my Father as nurturing; in retrospect, maybe even meant that way by Mother.

I N BETWEEN THE months of desperation, my Father and Mother, walking leaning slightly on one another, arm in arm, in a late fall afternoon. Mother is about thirty-eight and she is wearing a coat of cheap brown fur but she looks lovely in it. She wears brown opera pumps. Her hair is mid-length and brown, set in a casual style that complements her slightly squared face. My Father has on his hat, gray with a darker gray band, which he always wears, a charcoal coat and dark shoes. He holds Mother's arm in his protectively and they continue down the street lined with a few thin trees. Their faces are relaxed and they do not speak, even to chat, nor do they continue their unfinished quarrels. I sit on the fire escape, eight years old, doing homework, watching them dignified by their closeness.

Weekends, evenings, go by gently. Watching shows like *You Bet Your Life* with Groucho, *The Hit Parade* and *The Ed Sullivan Show* on our seven-inch black and white television, the lights down and the couch comfortable. My Father, sitting on the left, leaning on the side of the maroon couch, Mother next to him, leaning on his chest, and me on the end, feet curled up on the sofa, snuggling into Mother's arms. Hardly caring what is showing on the screen. Taking in the moments of peace and contentment, gaining strength from them to withstand the coming pressures. Feeling solid, feeling included in a unit, having a taste of the treasures found in a good family. Getting a sample that would make us yearn for the goodness, moments of closeness and quiet communication we once shared. Giving me a base to work from to have this enrichment, not just on occasion but as a daily nourishment, as I felt in my heart it could be.

My Father, Mother and I, walking along the Coney Island boardwalk, among thousands of people but intrinsically alone. Little conversation, always little conversation. Would we not have been better off with some talk of the oppressions of the weeks? Yes, but still I recall and cherish those days, walking easily together along the boardwalks, streets, parks, shores of the city in harmony of a sort difficult to convey or duplicate. We would stop for ice cream, full of raspberries or pecans, thick and whipped and flowing over sugar cones; and thin, light pizza slices, hot and saucy out of the oven, with mozzarella cheese sizzling on them, counting out four or five pieces of red dried hot peppers. And sometimes cotton candy, floating in pink swirls, evaporating in our mouths like steam or smoke, then play-fighting with the now empty paper cones.

Then stopping at the Penny Arcade, trying to make the bumper cars stay on the road as they moved in random maddening directions; playing skeeball, winding the balls at an angle down the alley to hit the side and fall straight into the holes, each higher and higher and higher and smaller and smaller, as the point value increased. My Father consistently getting the high forties and fifties, Mother flubbing it more often than not, and me trying valiantly and with some success to come near to my Father's score. Saving coupons for years, and never using them, for the places went out of business before we ever collected our winnings, but it did not matter for we had our stash which grew steadily larger and more exciting, and it was worth its value in fantasy.

And there was Nathan's, where a gaunt Italian man with vitality and sweat running down his face would recognize me each year, conspiring with me in the game of smiling sweetly to get what he said were the most luscious frankfurters, their skin dark brown and split open. My Father would send me through the heavy crowd to get franks for us all, agreeing that I could get the best ones, and he and Mother would wait by the fire hydrant as the crowd jostled them back and forth while I milled my way through the mass of people intent on their own orders. Once in a while we would go into the back room and eat at a table, giving the waiter our order, sometimes fried shrimp in a cup or hot chopped lobster salad on a bun; and lots of fries, and a fishwich sandwich to give us more quantity and cut down on the expense. We often had to wait a half-hour or more before finding seats and we stood silently by the door, feeling affluent as we watched the wealthier people at the tables relishing their informal meals.

Moments. Rare, precious moments.

SIRENS, SIRENS, SCREECHING in the night. The sound flooding through bones and teeth, into skulls, tearing at the eyes. My Father sleeping, snoring softly on the white, ironed sheets, his face strained in the small hall light. Mother tiptoeing out of bed, hushing me into the foyer and the kitchen. Waiting. Hearing the sirens close their screams and the car relax. Steps, steps up to our door. No. Not yet, please not yet. Mother opens the door and they come into the kitchen. She shows them the papers, signed by two doctors. I bite my fingernails and wait. And still my Father sleeps, snoring softly in his heavy dreams.

They approve of the papers. They are large men, not unkind looking. They have done this before and are not heroes nor are they hardened. Matter of factly, they ask if Mother wants to go in to wake him or if they should. She hesitates, then says that she will. He is not dangerous or anything, she explains, but would probably get pretty upset. She walks back into the bedroom and the policemen and I remain silently in the kitchen, the police taking out cigarettes, sitting around the green flowered tablecloth.

We hear some mumbling. I know Mother is trying to be firm and not show her fear and indecision. Some rustling and low conversation. I am chewing my nails as if I could swallow my hands whole. Suddenly my Father is there. He is dressed neatly in a white shirt open at the collar and suit pants; Mother is still in an old maroon robe.

"Hello, I'm S-S-S-Sam Levy, how are you doing?" My Father puts out his hand to the closest policeman who has stood up to meet him.

"Fine," answers the cop, taken aback by his apparent good nature and essentially healthy appearance. "You?"

"Good," my Father says. "Sorry about stuttering just now. I don't do it very often. Only when I talk." Conspiratorial smile to the two policemen. They grin back. Mother looks ragged in her old robe, anxious and depressed.

"What's the story, anyway?" my Father asks.

"Well, it's like this, sir. We've got papers here, you know, and we've got to . . ."

Do I only remember it this way? I was so young. Were they really startled at his composure, despite his stuttering; unnerved at his gentle frankness? I know they looked over the papers again, and apologized to my Father, looked quizzically at Mother and me.

And were they wrong to suspect the doctors' judgment? Could my Father, given time and understanding, have gathered together his thoughts and dreams and somehow made it out of the crisis without being incarcerated in the deathlike steel place, without being drugged past sensibility, without having unresolved memories shocked out of him, without compassion or choice?

So much being done with chemicals in this enlightened age, to control loosened thoughts, to limit incongruous behavior. But are there no alternatives?

What would my Father be like today, had someone held him gently and accepted his pent-up fears, or shown him ways to reach out and gain what he could not obtain by himself instead of taking him into the backroom of the hospital, lining him up, and laying him like an animal roughly down on the steel chair, placing rubber clamps on his head and above his ears, and sending jolts of electricity painfully, mercilessly through his brain, without his consent or approval, tying him down in a fist of contempt and brutality?

Is it easier now than it was then, now that it does not hurt physically as it once did? Is it less brutal, less cruel, now that it blocks out sections of the mind painlessly and swiftly? Do people know, do they know, that the chance of recurrence of the manic cycle increases with shock treatment and that the person, unless he is one of the lucky ones who changes permanently, (perhaps to avoid the aversive thing) is more likely to deteriorate after shock than without it, never able to express the feelings endured over years of unhappiness?

Where would my Father be now had they let him go free?

Do they know of this:
> that the ravings of a maniac, his terror and tears,
> can be stilled
> with the shock of a human heart
> better than the shock of wires;
> with the chemistry in the eyes
>> of one who cares
> better than the chemistry of drugs;
> with the restraint of the nuances
>> of your mouth
> better than the restraint of an
>> old shirt, tied from behind.

WE USED TO take long rides into the country, or what seemed like country, compared to the Brooklyn streets. We always had a car; even while in debt my Father would invariably find a great used car to buy, through some fantastic deal. We had a Hudson, a Buick, a Chevrolet. Cars were one thing that my Father had the ultimate control and say over. Mother couldn't drive and wouldn't learn, which was typical for women in those days. It worked well for our family—the overwhelming sense was of my Father's impending if not actual failure—he needed any competencies he could gather.

My Father knew every car on the road, model number, year, details, from the front, side, rear. He probably would have known it from overhead or under—though he knew nothing mechanically. He taught me patiently the names and styles and by the time I was eight I knew most of them, and he would show me off when anyone else was around. It made driving for long hours fun and I never got sick or tired or bored when we drove together. Car identifying was supplemented by other games, like finding the most taxis, buses, trucks, old men, signposts, and stray animals.

Sometimes we would find a place to stop and Mother would take out a picnic basket of sandwiches and potato salad or pieces of roast chicken, and we would pour salt all over whatever came out of the bags, getting covered with grease and mayonnaise and ketchup—even Mother at times participating unchecked. These weekends seemed the sweetest times, a respite between the drudgery of other days and the terror of other nights.

I wish I could have understood at the time what was happening to our small world when it went upside down. It was a great mystery, shrouded in despair and intensity. Mental illness, relationship problems, were not dealt with openly. Rather than admit that there was something wrong, we moved to another apartment on another street, and kept our secrets limited to hushed phone calls, allusions and behind closed doors, until violence and emotion eventually erupted through the suppression.

IT IS DIFFICULT to remember when I first found out that my Father was what society and the doctors and my mother called crazy. I know that Mother said that my friend at camp had a father who was crazy, as distinguished from me who had a Father who had had a nervous breakdown. That is, her father was really nuts, whereas my Father only had a problem. This was also a problem to be kept secret at all costs. My Father would scream as if his brain would split trying to make Mother understand how he felt, and she would be furious, not at his words, or his tone or his demands, but at the thought of the neighbors hearing his voice in the apartments down the hall. As if they did not know that we were coming apart from within with no control; as if they cared.

I never told a soul. I never thought to tell. It was something I carried with me every day. I would see people's fathers and know they were whole, and yet would think that my Father was better than them, and I would always think how glad I was I had my Father, with his gentle humor and wondrous silver-blue eyes and endless patience with me in my fears.

One day I broke this pact of secrecy. I had had a homework assignment for class and my Father was very high the night before and I had not done the work. My Father and Mother had been fighting way into the night. The next morning I went to school and when the teacher called on me for a response based on the homework I had none. I was instructed to write "I will do my homework" five hundred times, and also hand in the homework by the next day, but what distressed me was that I was aware of how bad he thought I was for not doing what I was supposed to do. When the class let out I dawdled in my seat getting papers together while he was gathering papers on his desk. Everyone had left and I began to shake, could not stop the trembling. Yet I went over to his desk and faced him. His complexion was grayed and sallow and he had not shaved. He was not a happy man and did not take care of himself properly, though he could not have been more than forty years old.

"I want to tell you why I didn't have my homework . . ." I said to him, not looking at him, but seeing his loose skin by his jaws and his hostile eyes behind the thick glasses he glared through.

"Well?" he said abruptly.

"It's my Father," I began, unable to stop shaking, unable to stop my words which I knew I should control. I pictured him removing his glasses and his eyes changing to kindness. I pictured him putting his arm gently around my shoulder and saying softly, "Oh, I'm sorry. I'm so sorry." He would forgive me for not doing my homework, would understand the pain of the night before, the pain of the long, incomprehensible years.

"He . . . he's had a breakdown. He and my mother were screaming all night, and I—I just couldn't do my homework . . ." I kept my eyes on his desk, trembling, how I could not stop the trembling.

I was aware that he was still putting his things in his briefcase. Then I was aware that he was further away. And then I saw that he had left, that I was alone by his desk, alone in the room, standing by his gray metal desk, trembling, alone and trembling.

THINGS WOULD APPEAR to be going along fairly routinely, when in a matter of hours my Father's eyes would change from their gentle silver-blue softness and begin to glaze over. His face would sweat more and his smile would become too intense. His arms would not lie correctly at his sides but would seem to move as if fastened too tightly at the elbows, his whole arm from the shoulder moving when only his arms or hands should have moved. He would need only two or three hours of sleep at night and wake up as intense and excitable as when he went to bed—my Father, who would ordinarily sleep ten hours easily and deeply. Then would begin his preoccupation with learning several things at once. He would ask me to borrow books for him from school or the library and I would and even try to go over lessons with him, but he would become frustrated at the first few words and go back to endlessly speaking of all the things he planned to do.

He would begin questioning religions and God during these periods, something he would always avoid at other times. He would go over to people on the street and ask what they thought of their religion and get them into a discussion. I would hold onto my Father's arm in awe at his nerve, directness and sociability. People would find this interesting at first but soon he would challenge the basis of their beliefs and we would be in for a street quarrel. He would begin joking when people were in dead earnest and take minor jokes as offense, so I never knew exactly what to expect when we went out together. During these periods, however, he made me feel as if I were his closest friend and I would follow him around feeling, alternately, pride and embarassment.

The really damaging things my Father did at these times, from Mother's point of view, were related to money. Money had no value in itself to him, though Mother was scrimping to make ends meet as his low-paying jobs were short-lived and her salary as a woman at the Board of Education, despite her doing upper level work, was stable but small. When my Father was high, he would bring home trinkets for Mother and me, little items that were curious but of no utilitarian value. I remember our mantle covered with blown glass figurines that he had impulsively bought during manic states. We had glass swans, elephants, giraffes, flowers, flamingos, boats, jewelry, a lighthouse, and the blown glass merry-go-round that I imagined moving to music, as I sat alone dreaming by the never-lit fireplace. He bought candy boxes in all sizes and shapes for me and Mother, wallets, knick-knacks, bracelets, clothing in odd sizes. But these were the small things. The large items that got us in debt were the car for which he wrote an $800 check that bounced and Mother had to pay for, several expensive coats, furniture, sets of dishes, encyclopedias. Not only that but he would mock Mother by tearing up dollar bills right before her eyes, later pacifyng her by taping the less damaged ones back together.

Between his highs and lows, he went sporadically from welding to selling to cooking to various independent ventures, back and forth through unskilled trades. Selling seemed to be what he did the most and possibly even enjoyed. When he was selling Wearever products, he would speak to groups of potential customers, bringing along free sandwiches as part of the sales technique. We would make the sandwiches early in the mornings for him to take to work. We would form an assembly line at the flowered green tablecloth, and one of us would lay out slices of white bread, then ham or salami, sliced American cheese, lettuce, slap on mustard or mayonnaise on the top white bread slice and carefully close up the sandwiches. My Father would cut them diagonally, and then carefully wrap them in waxed paper so they looked neat and professionally made.

These were some of the sweetest times, as my Father would joke and tickle us while we worked, and even Mother would relax as she counted and laid out slices of meat and cheese. But my Father was not very good as a salesman; the days of good hauls were far exceeded by the days of sandwiches given away for nothing. Mother used to say that he wasn't "cut out" to be a salesman, he was basically too honest, and also he took losses and gains personally, and I think she was right. I think shyness was part of the reason he never quite fit in that role. Also, he would get mixed feelings about whether or not he should be spending his time doing this when he had other abilities, if he could pinpoint what they were, and Mother fed this fantasy because of her own hopes. Mother married my Father with the assumption that he would return to school at night, at least long enough to finish high school, but in reality he never wanted to and never did.

I T WAS FATHER'S Day and I went from store to store looking for the perfect card to buy for my Father. My hair was straight and tangled from being twisted in my fingers, or chewed between my teeth. My hand-me-down clothes never fit correctly or went together right. I walked into stores with my head low, and my posture sloped, wanting to find a card for my Father that he would cherish. He would come over to me and ask, "What's this?" and I would shyly hand him my card, the one I finally picked out, soft lavender crocuses and irises in a bouquet, small leaves and swirls of brown-green, and in fine curved type, *Happy Father's Day.* And inside, the poem that said what I had in my heart to say to my Father, that I loved him more than anything in the world; that I thought he was special in a way no other Father could ever compare with. He would take the card gently from my fingers and slowly draw it out of the envelope on which I had scrawled, "I love you, Daddy" and he would smile at me, and how his face would light up when he saw the delicate colors and the elegant design. He would put his arm around me, bending down to my height as he opened the card and read the loving lines. How his face would shine, in the way it used to shine as he joked that I must have picked up the wrong card by mistake. "Uh, uh," I would deny, embarrassed, and he would lift me up and give me a bear hug and forget all his troubles and failures for the few precious moments we would have.

How I cherished the card I bought two weeks before Father's Day. I carried it with me to school and looked at it under my desk as the teacher's voice droned on. Finally the day arrived, and I took Mother's arm and went with her to the bus stop to get the Clarkson Avenue bus to go to the hospital. I could hardly contain my excitement at seeing him as I had not seen him for more than a month. Mother spoke to me constantly on the way to the hospital. She was anxious about us going and about my excitement that she picked up beneath my silence. She tried to explain to me that my Father was very depressed, that he was becoming very quiet and was content to sit around and think his sad thoughts. She told me she did not think he would talk much to us, and that she doubted that anything could make him feel better. And she went on about her thoughts and her own nervousness. I should have listened more closely, for I would have expected less from him, but I did not believe it could be true. I knew she always thought the worst about anything, and that she did not know how to love deeply, she was so involved with herself. I knew she did not have the patience with him that he needed, could not give him the tenderness he yearned for. How, then, could I have believed the coldness of her words? I knew him so much more than she did, inside where it mattered. There was so much love inside of him that he would open up like a flower on a spring-warm day when he saw my feelings given to him in quiet totality. He would lift me in his arms and smile as he had not smiled for so long.

I waited on the hospital grounds, sitting on a wooden bench near the entrance as Mother walked into the hall. He was better than he'd been, and they told Mother that he would come down to us by himself, so she waited with me on the bench in the warm sun, nervously fixing my hair which was quite beyond fixing, and straightening her pink tailored suit over her firm stockinged legs. Finally we saw him at the door and we walked over to him, he toward us. Mother was first and he kissed her on her mouth. I stood by him and waited for him to see me, hands trembling holding the lovely lavender card. How could it be that he did not notice me standing there, trembling in anticipation of being held in his arms? Mother extricated herself from him and spoke, said that I had a card for him for Father's Day that I wanted to give him and he looked at me blankly for a quick moment, not meeting my eyes. He shook his head and turned as if he did not understand what she had said to him.

My heart pounding in my chest, and seeing lights glazing in front of me, I stepped toward him, and tried to hand him the card. But he waved his hand in front of it and unsmiling moved away. Mother went with him and spoke to him but I saw my Father shake his head and go on. I stood there not believing, and Mother turned and shrugged without quite meeting my eyes, as they walked down the path. I turned abruptly and sat back down on the bench and waited. Until visiting time was over, I waited for my Father, and when it was over he went straight back up to the ward, never saying good-bye to me. He never came back to say good-bye.

I SPEAK TO Mother about the past; inevitably I offer her a voice. After all, she probably knows more about it than anyone, although part of me denies it. I have vague remembrances about a bread route, the bread route that there was so much bitterness around. Tell me about it, Mother.

"That was so awful," Mother says, "I can hardly remember it. Most of it is blocked from my memory. How I could have been so stupid as to believe your father, I'll never know.

"This guy he'd never laid eyes on before sold him a bread route . . . for $1200! $1200! He couldn't have gotten twelve cents from anyone else. It was for a route somewhere in Far Rockaway. You were supposed to deliver orders—challah, rye bread, pumpernickel, rolls, bagels, even lox and cream cheese, to people's homes.

"Your father didn't even get a truck or a van for the money. Nothing tangible. That's what's so ridiculous about the whole thing. All he got was 'goodwill,' what they called the referrals. All we got for $1200—I'd earned that money by the sweat of my brow and borrowed for it, too—was a list of names from the other guy's delivery list.

"I should have known better. But this guy convinced your father and he convinced me. Your father was manic then already. I didn't recognize the symptoms—I should have, but I didn't. Boy, was I stupid.

"So your father was supposed to deliver all this stuff, in our car, naturally, early in the morning when it was still dark so people could have it fresh when they woke up, but right from the beginning he didn't follow through and deliver what he was supposed to. He didn't get up in time and he made mistakes in the orders. It was impossible from the beginning. Your father got more and more confused and agitated and eventually he said he would only deliver things if I went with him, and for a while I did, even though I had to go to work right after, with hardly any sleep. But I hated to see all that money thrown away.

"I'll never forget the last day of the bread route. He was definitely manic by then. He was screaming, getting into fights with people, and this was practically in the middle of the night. People were threatening to call the cops. He was speeding, driving on two wheels, giving me the bread to deliver at his stops. I couldn't stand it—I had no control over him. Finally he left me at one stop. Just drove off after I told him he was sick and needed to go back to Brooklyn State. He said, 'You're crazy, not me,' and left me standing there. The man we were delivering food to had woken up and was there when he left and I told him, 'He's sick, I've got to help him.' I'll never forget what he said: 'What are you worrying about him for? Take care of yourself. Be glad he left.' He even got me a ride home—a cab or a friend—I can't remember.

"The next night I pulled up the shade in the hall after your father fell asleep, as a signal to Pauline—remember her, she also had a husband with a lot of mental problems—and she called the police for me and we finally got him back in Brooklyn State."

M Y BEST FRIEND Diane's father, Jack, a calm, redheaded man with gold-rimmed glasses, suddenly became high strung, angry and irritable. His doctor prescribed medication for high blood pressure and later gave him antibiotics when he discovered he had a urinary infection. But by the time he was correctly diagnosed with kidney failure, it was too late.

Jack's sudden temper outbursts and frequent intrusions into my private adolescent conversations with Diane would get me very nervous, and my nervousness translated into hysterical laughter. Jack would get furious at my laughter, certain I was laughing at him. I used to feel terrible guilt when I saw him, especially when we learned that he was seriously ill.

My Father and I used to spend a lot of time at Diane's do-what-ever-you-like home, to escape Mother's rigidity. So the day Jack began to pass out in pain, my Father, who was hanging out, singing fifties songs with Diane's brother at the piano, was the logical one to drive Jack to the hospital. For some reason, my Father wanted Diane and me to go with them and we sat in the back seat while Jack sat next to my Father, his face red, holding cotton up his nose to stop the bleeding that had begun.

I was anxious and upset during the drive and I could not control my hysterical giggling, although I tried to muffle it with my hands. My Father told me sharply to be quiet, but Jack said in a calm and uncannily clear voice: "She is just a child. It is all right." Hearing his soft voice was a great relief to me and I relaxed, feeling that Jack wanted me to know that he understood and forgave me.

That was one of the most careful rides I have ever taken. My Father drove slowly and was in every way considerate of Jack, and gentle as anyone could have been. But two days later, the once vital young man was dead, and a short while later my Father, great in an emergency but depleted of his emotional reserves, was committed to the Third Floor, East Wing of the Ward.

MY FATHER'S OLDER sister, my Aunt Ruth, always brought sandwiches when she visited at the hospital—homemade chopped liver, chicken with celery and mayonnaise, pastrami, or thick slices of brisket on Jewish rye bread. She would bring enough for all of us and my Father and I and sometimes Mother would share the small feast. Aunt Ruth was generous with the little money she had, sending all of us three or four dollar bills for birthday presents through the mail faithfully each year.

We would sit out on the porch area of the third floor, crowded with other visiting families, looking through the fencing at the people outside. If my Father was very depressed, he would not speak at all, except to nod his head and perhaps whisper fine if we asked him more than once how he was. Mother sometimes spoke of her work or held his hand and Aunt Ruth would talk about her thyroid condition or her other health problems. Before we got to the hospital and while we were there I obsessed over what I could say to my Father that would evoke a response.

When Mother and he were separated and he was compliant enough to go out alone on a pass, I would take the subway to meet him on Sundays. My preoccupation with how to have a conversation grew worse at these times because we would have interminable periods of silence, which would paralyze me for days after.

We would go to Coney Island on the warm days when he was in Brooklyn State and also after he was released, during the times he lived alone in a cheap rooming house in the city until he had proved to Mother that he was "ready" to come home, a vague standard that included having a menial job and being appropriately submissive.

We would walk along the boardwalk, past rides and games and food, and sit for a long while on wooden folding chairs, listening silently to the auctioneer pushing steak knives, razors, or stockings, without ever buying anything, my Father convinced it was all a rip-off. When the auction was over, we would take some newspapers out of a wastebasket, and sit on a bench for a long time looking through them, still not speaking. I had so many thoughts that I never dared let out. I remember taking a notebook and writing some of my feelings down, feeling I would suffocate with words in my throat.

Sometimes we would go down to the beach and I would lie down with the sun on me and he would then lie down, too, his head on my stomach, putting the newspaper pages over his eyes and fall asleep, time passing with no direction or purpose. What can I say to my Father when he wakes up that would matter, I would think, over and over. It seemed there was nothing that could be said that would break through the thin shield of normalcy we worked so hard to fabricate, and so I remained dumb, yearning to speak. I knew some of his feelings, the exhaustion, hopelessness, dependency, the overwhelming sense of failure. But how to speak with him of these: this I never knew, or could, or did.

SCENE:

AN ABOVE-GROUND SUBWAY station on the BMT line, Brooklyn, New York, 1955. There are a few people around—an elderly woman sitting on a bench, two teenagers talking by a pole, a man standing reading the paper. The afternoon sun is warm and the usual subway smells are minimal. Residential buildings can be seen in the distance to the left of the platform.

A young girl with straight, long, thin yellow hair and glasses, in a white blouse and navy skirt, her school clothing, with a worried look, and a man in his forties, in a blue shirt, gray pants, a jacket and red sneakers, jaunty, walk down the stairs at the back end, from under the signs that say Culver line and EXIT in black letters on a green background.

The father is talking nonstop to the young girl who is staying close to his side. He is clearly agitated. They wait for the train to arrive.

MAN
Hey, how close do you think I can get to the edge of the platform without falling over the edge?

GIRL
(Caught off-guard)
What?

MAN

Don't what me. What do you think?

Without waiting for an answer, the man moves toward the edge of the platform.

GIRL

Daddy....

The girl moves slowly toward him till she is on his left, but a step further from the platform.

MAN

Daddy what?

GIRL

I'm sure you can get really close. You don't have to prove it.

MAN

I'm not trying to prove anything. I'm just asking. How close?

His red sneakers move to the edge of the platform. He stands there for a moment and then gradually moves his foot inch by inch closer to the tracks below.

GIRL

(Strained but trying to remain calm externally.)
Daddy please just come back and talk to me.

MAN

Bet you're getting nervous now. Your mother telling you stories about the third rail hot as an electric chair. But it won't get me.

I've got balance. See?

The train light begins to be seen around the bend from a far distance. The sound can barely be heard. No one pays attention to the strange man and young girl at the back end of the station. This is New York.

GIRL

Ok, Daddy. You've proved your point and made me nervous. The train's coming—now can you please back up?

MAN

(His tone daring his daughter to do something)
Hey, the train's not even close.

Tears are in her eyes, the train is in clear sight, the screeching sound is getting louder, the whistle is beginning to blast in their ears, and the girl panics.

GIRL

You're right Daddy. You can do anything. And yes now I'm scared. Really scared. Please come back here. Just one or two steps back . . .

The man laughs triumphantly, puts his hand to his cheek, steps back from the track seconds before the train looms in front of him.

MAN

(Grandiose)

See you don't have to worry about me. I can outsmart anyone, even a train. And nobody tells Sam Levy what he can or can't do.

The girl, visibly shaken, lowers her eyes, says nothing.

MAN

Am I right or am I right?

GIRL

Yes, Daddy. You're right.

The train stops and the two go through the open doors of the last car, find a corner seat and ride toward the City, to spend the day walking the streets of Times Square.

I LISTEN IN horror to my Father and Mother arguing in the hospital.

"Damn it, Lil, how could you sign for shock treatments when you promised you wouldn't. You lied to me, damn you!"

"What are you talking about, Sam?"

"Twice they took me in. Twice!! And you tell me you don't know what I'm saying!"

"I don't understand. I didn't sign for anything. I swear I didn't, Sam!"

"You're lying, Lil!"

"I'm telling the truth. You're not supposed to be getting shock treatments."

"Well, I got them. Go look at my chart if you don't believe me. I told them I wasn't supposed to go but they wouldn't listen to me. You don't have any rights in a nuthouse."

"It must have been a mistake. An awful mistake."

"A mistake? A mistake? And I'm the one that's supposed to be crazy?"

And it was true. In black and white on the chart.

How could it have been? How can people make errors like that? On other people? On my Father?

Such indignities, such mortification, such ignorance and destruction. How did he survive it at all?

Another time; same place. My Father in his usual costume of gray/white when Mother and I come in, only this time he is lying on his back with white rags tying his hands and legs down to the sides of the bed. He is furious, enraged at being tied down.

"Will you open those goddamn ties, Lil!" he yells over and over, embarrassing Mother as his screams shoot down the hallways.

Mother comes closer to him and they negotiate. She will open the ties to his legs only, she says, so he can be more comfortable. He agrees to this, and she bends down to open the white cloth.

I watch the transaction from my usual passive state. No one else, despite Mother's fears, seems interested.

Finally the ties are loose. Mother is bent over my Father. Suddenly I see his foot strike out and land in Mother's side.

"Bitch," he says, "I have to beg you to untie my legs."

MY FATHER IS doing well and has been moved to the ground floor where patients can leave for the day as long as they return by 5:00. This Sunday, we meet at the 14th Street subway stop and walk toward the East Village. My Father is in a good mood and I am, too, and we decide to have an early lunch at the small corner restaurant we come to. We are the only ones there and the old man at the counter greets us, starts up a conversation.

"What I really love to do," confides the soft-spoken man in his seventies, "is play the violin."

"The violin?" my Father says, his mouth open in fascination, his hand on his cheek, eyes shining.

"Yes," the man says. "Always my dream has been to play the violin." "I bet you're a terrific violinist," my Father says.

"Eh, you know," the man says wistfully. "I bet you are," he assures him.

"C'mere a minute, mister. You bring your daughter, too. I have something I bring to the store here, and when it gets slow and there's no one here . . . well, you know."

"No," he says encouragingly, as we follow the man toward the back of the restaurant.

"Yah, really. Look, see, here she is." And in a moment a beautiful, old, well-cared-for violin appears on the counter between condiments, menus and place settings.

The man plays an old Russian melody for us, and then some songs from the thirties, and we sit there, enthralled by the spontaneous concert before us. The man invites us to sing along with him and we do until other customers come in and he puts the violin away and goes back to work. And he never questions what my Father does, where he lives, or what his diagnosis is.

A RARE OCCASION, having a friend over for dinner, but all I remember, besides my Father's affect which was slow and uncertain as if he were relearning how to function after too much medication and hospitalization, is the incident of the string beans.

Mother had cooked a pot roast and baked potatoes, leaving my Father in charge of the vegetable, which entailed simply opening up a can of string beans and putting them in a pan on the stove. That went all right, but just as we were about to sit down at the table, trying to be normal, Mother smelled something burning.

"The string beans!" she screamed, running over to the stove. "I ask you to do one thing, ONE THING and you can't even do that right," she yelled at my Father, forgetting me, forgetting my friend, forgetting he had just come out of the hospital, forgetting everything but the string beans that she knew were completely ruined.

My Father never answered her. He looked down at the ground like a small child who was ashamed, ashamed of what he had done and ashamed of what he was. He stood there humiliated while Mother took off the salvageable beans and served them up and put cold water in the burnt pan. He stood there until Mother returned in the silence and, in burning shame, we all sat down to eat.

ONE OF THE most satisfying and meaningful periods of my Father's life had to have been the summer when I was fifteen and he was forty-three. He was second chef at a camp in the Pocono Mountains and for the last part of the summer I was hired as a counselor for a small group of eight-year-old girls. Willie, the main chef, took a liking to my Father and under his good-humored instructions my Father had a summer of success. The kitchen staff worked seven days a week from 6:00 a.m. till late at night, with few breaks, but my Father seemed to thrive in this environment, in a job that was fair and kept him busy, even if it wasn't easy or glamorous. Willie saw the goodness and sensitivity beneath my Father's tired near-despair and in an atmosphere of easy teasing and open appreciation my Father relaxed and seemed to thrive.

Sometimes, during afternoon breaks, we found time to walk down to the lake or take a short hike in the woods. My Father listened to me, even to my poems, uncritically, simply and affectionately. He talked about himself only in jokes or generalities, but I could see he was happier here than I had ever seen him in a constant, stable way, or would again.

In the evenings the waiters, college kids working for the summer, would invite him to go bowling with them and often he would go and sometimes I would come with him. It was a game he enjoyed and was good at, frequently making spares and strikes.

People there liked and respected my Father. I saw it in the way they spoke to him. His gentleness and humor came through to them, and his quick mind.

At summer's end, Willie wanted him to work with him somewhere else, but my Father never followed up. Why did he let it slip away? A section of time, less than three months when he was accepted, working, capable and making a good life for himself. Why did it stop? I cannot believe that is the way he wanted it. The moments, the hours were too good to have been purposely discarded by him.

All I have left of these days are letters my Father wrote to me during the month before I joined him from another camp nearby. Three letters I treasure, letters filled with humor, affection and gentleness.

Letters From My Father

July, 1958

Dear Shauna,

Everything is going along good here at Camp Weeq—Camp Weq—Camp Wag—er in Lakewood! Since I help to cook for about 170 people, 3 new hospitals were organized. Anyway, it's nice up here. It's about 3 miles from Winona. I went bowling with the boss's son and a couple of the waiters. Age 17 to 18. I am forwarding in the next mail 3 dozen pictures of each. Not that you would be interested or anything! I work 7 days a week but I get off every 2 months. So I should have a day off some time in August, probably 2 days <u>after</u> I leave camp.

How are you making out? Are the little infants giving you a hard time? Remember to hold your temper and don't spank them! Use a brick instead! And I don't mean an Ice Cream Brick either! Write A.S.A.P.

With Love and Kisses, Your
Fawthaw, Head Chef, Waldorf
Astoria Hotel

P.S. I was going to send you some money but I forgot to put it in the envelope.

*The lady on the stamp on the envelope must be really in love with him. Look at the torch she is carrying!

July, 1958

My Dearest Daughter,

I received your letter a few days ago and it was the best letter I have ever received from anyone outside of Mommy. I could not answer right away because we had the parents over for a <u>free</u> meal so you know what happened, they ate themselves sick. One of the camper's father said, I'll have my cow as is. Last weekend we cooked for 370 people and it took until Tuesday to straighten out the joint. To top it all 2 waiters left. One quit, one got fired! We just hired our fourth pot washer. One a week. Just like a pill. Willie and I had to peel onions, dice celery, grind meat, etc. in addition to our other duties of which we had plenty. Things started to calm down to a roar today so I was able to send letters to you, Ma and Aunt Ruth.

Otherwise things are going along pretty fair so far. The boss has not complained about my work so far. He spent the past 3 weeks in the infirmary. TOENAIL poisoning.

By the way how are you making out with the painting of Diane? Send me the item about the storm!

At the lake here it has rained about 19 days out of 24. I told a couple of the waiters what a charming daughter I have and they are anxious to meet you—could be! Is there anything new at the camp? What age group are you taking care of now? Has the food improved? How do you feel? I am writing this letter as the children are walking in and here is a candid word picture of a charming child camper at Camp Weequahic, "WHAT? THAT GARBAGE AGAIN?"

Love and Kisses
From your Daddy

*The little brats are now lined up waiting for food as I close this letter with the old saying: Camps are camps but

I'll bet you would like to be home now and listen to a little yelling from your mother? I saw a picture called "Hot Spell" which wasn't so <u>Hot</u>.

> So long till next time
> Daddy

July, 1958

Dear Shauna,

Glad to hear from you. I had sent one letter and spent about 2 1/2 hours trying to call you last week and so I think I did my part. I am very busy up here as I start in working at about 6:15 a.m. and sometimes at 8:30 p.m. I am still working. P.S. I don't accomplish anything, but boy can I work! Today we had fried eggs and the shells got nice and brown. Tomorrow we expect to open them! For lunch we had brisket of beef, string beans and a free meal ticket to the <u>Automat</u>. Last Friday I went to a movie. I saw Debbie Reynolds in "This Happy Feeling." When I left I had a <u>Miserable Feeling</u>.

The picture was so bad that a robber held up the box office and said to the cashier, "Give me everybody's money back" and she did!

It was a typical picture of an average American family. He had a 34-room house with 12 baths, 4 cars, 3 garages and a maid for each arm. She was a secretary with an empty closet of 68 dresses, 42 bras, 93 slips, 140 sweaters, 226 pairs of shoes and one little measly mink! And they think they are having trouble in Europe!

I also went bowling one night with the boss's son and my scores were 184 and 146. His scores were 132 and 117. After I got fired—He is 21. He has a girl friend. You are: 1. prettier, 2. nicer, 3. more stacked, 4. better personality and what's more important you have a far more intelligent father.

In our place we have a baker. 70 years old. Saturday he turned on the oven and then looked for a match. BOOM! He found the match. He was really a nice man. Seriously he wasn't hurt very badly. Just got third degree burns. He will be out for 2 days. I heard Diane has Poison Ivy. Is she over it yet or does it last more than 3 or 4 days? Tell me more about the camp. How many kids? What kind of recreation (boys) is there also what do you do in your spare time (boys) or do you go in for any hobby (boys)?

Love & Kisses from your
Second Cook

P.S. When you write you can't do wrong!

P.S.S. Please wash the stamp in the washing machine, hang it out to dry and send it back to me. Times are Tough! Your Skotch Daddy.

D ID I DO this to my Father? Am I less to blame because I was
still a child?

Did I do this to my Father, a continuing buffer between Mother
and me when I was hurt, who kept my fears from growing too large to
handle, giving a swift dose of reality to exaggerated fears amplified by
Mother's anxieties. "I scraped my knee—it's bleeding!" Mother hysterical, running around getting band-aids and iodine, talking too loud, long,
fast, acting as if I would shortly bleed to death. "Now look what you did
to the sidewalk," my Father would say, importantly, and I would auto-
matically stop crying to view the injured walk, then catch his eyes with
their impish smile and laugh knowing I was all right and whole again.

Did I do this to my Father, who spared me when he could the
awful ordeals of breakfast? Food, so much food, Mother trying to
force me to eat whether I was hungry or not, whether I wanted to eat
or not, whether I liked the food or not.

My Father was no match for Mother, but sometimes he would
come over and interrupt her nagging and hassling me to drink my
orange juice and say, "That's all right, Lil. Let her be. I'll see to it that
she drinks it." Then he would sit by me and talk with me patiently,
about anything at all, maybe joke around, and then he would say
casually, "Hey, I'm gonna make a bet with you, and I bet you'll lose."
What kind of bet I would want to know, and perhaps he would say,
"I bet you can'tdrink that orange juice all up by the time the second
hand reaches the twelve again. What do you say? Is it a bet?" Well,
turned out I didn't hate the juice that much if I wasn't coerced into
drinking it, so down would go all the orange juice, in way less than
the minute that he had given me, and he would throw his hands up
in mock amazement. A sweet game, with no losers.

Did I do this to my Father, who wrote a breathtaking message on the back of my class picture, using the first four initials of my favorite song "Love Is A Many Splendored Thing" to begin it? His words that I hold in my heart: "Love Is A Must, far, far more important than the Yankee dollar, which cannot kiss one back."

Yes, he was high and argumentative, had been irritating and hostile on the streets and in restaurants, a public nuisance, volatile and unpredictable. And yes, he had been spending money we didn't have to spend. But he was in the same time span loving and understanding.

How many nights did I stay awake after, haunted by repeats of the scene, haunted by my Father's eyes as he turned and saw what he saw?

WE WERE OVER Diane's house as we were so often, escaping the rigidity of our house. My Father was standing by the piano in the den, in his hoarse, funny voice singing with Diane and her mother the songs of the fifties, Diane's brother, Irwin on the keys. The scene quaint and tender, out of an Elizabethan novel. He was relaxed and comfortable; the frenzied look indiscernible in his silver-blue eyes.

I had left the room, to call the police. It was almost a week since Mother had given me the papers signed by two doctors to keep in my junk-filled purse, with instructions to wait until the right time presented itself to call.

But I was the one who chose the time, because it seemed easy. And, in all fairness, no one forced me to make the move.

I called them to take my Father away to be committed and he was so preoccupied with singing and reminiscing, he did not perceive me leave the room, go into the bedroom and make the call.

When the bell rang and they came into the hall he couldn't see them, so he continued at the piano as Diane's mother and I spoke to them, showing them quietly into the kitchen. I gave them the papers signed by two psychiatrists and they prepared to go in and return my Father to the hospital, which he had been out of for over two years.

When they came in his face lost its color and he stopped singing as he met their eyes. "Just want to finish this song," he said, after a moment. "Just want to finish this song." Diane's brother began to play again at a signal from my Father and Diane continued singing with him. The police went back in the kitchen to wait.

I stayed in the dining room, neither thinking nor feeling. When the song was finished my Father came over to me. His face was strained. "Who called them?" he asked me, and I could not look at him. "You?" he asked, suddenly suspicious, and I nodded my head in admission. His face changed then to hatred and he doubled up his fist as if to hit out at me and I pulled away in fear, though in truth the only time he had ever hit me was when I was six years old and started to run out into the street without looking first to check for traffic, and for the next hour until it disappeared treasured his handprint on my thigh as a symbol of his love.

I ran into the kitchen where the police were standing and sat down. Soon my Father came in, composed again, and he stated in a flat voice that he was ready to go.

A WEDDING, SUMMER, 1960. My Father at the edge of becoming high again. Intervals between episodes had been steadily decreasing. Years later, as a social work student, I read that this is one of the long-term effects of shock treatments.

The past few months I had tried out being Bohemian, wearing dark clothing and putting my hair back in a tight bun. In my own world, having taken on the persona of a withdrawn intellectual, I wore a plain black dress to the wedding and thought I looked interesting if not pretty in black-framed glasses and a sullen look. Mother was wearing something nondescript but appropriate and was edgy with anxiety.

My cousin Dolores, nineteen, two years older than I, was getting married. Beautiful and modern, in her fluffy, low cut, lacy whiteness setting off her heavy tanned exuberance, she barely said hello to me. Her bridesmaids, dressed in lavender, pink and orange netted gowns, were seated at a table with their boyfriends. They danced and talked and laughed. How strange we must have seemed to them, me especially in my black dress, gradually realizing how odd I looked as the night wore on.

It was a hot stuffy room, with a lot of people and too much food. My Father was not clearly high; only Mother and I suspected subtle differences in his eyes and walk. After we drank some wine, Mother and I, (my Father contained his own high), we felt more part of the whole and began to relax.

The best part of the wedding, for my Father, came in the middle of the evening. The band was playing and people were dancing and my Father and his brother Joe requested the band play songs they knew. My Father seemed to fit in with the festive mood and he and

Joe put their arms around Herbie, the father of the bride, and with some harmony and effect sang old time songs. I remember my Father sweating and his face glowing with wetness, singing, "Let Me Call You Sweetheart," passion and tenderness in his peculiar, hoarse voice. "Let me call you sweetheart—I'm in love with you." Affectionately standing, arms intertwined, the three of them sang nostalgically of love: all three of them men disappointed in love and marriage. Singing longingly and movingly of romance.

The wedding went on, getting hotter and hotter and noisier.

Suddenly a voice from the back called out something we did not understand and a few people started walking toward the lobby, set off from the main area. Mother told my Father to sit down, but he ignored her and I followed him.

A man was slumped on the bench, his face discolored and ashen. A few people had begun gathering, seemingly in shock.

"Someone call an ambulance," we heard and my Father took charge, found a phone in the corridor and called, composed in his movements. He told everyone authoritatively to move away from the man and keep calm. Dolores' mother walked over in her heavy rose dress and her short kinky hair, and didn't recognize the man. "C'mon, this is a party, c'mon, let's go and dance," she said. Almost everyone followed her back to the party and there were only three or four of us left.

No one seemed to know this man, a heavy-set middle-aged man who had collapsed from the heat and was sprawled on the wooden bench. I watched his face for movement, and suddenly thought, maybe he's dead, and whispered it out loud but I couldn't be heard above the band's refrains in the background.

The ambulance came quickly and the men came in with their stretcher to the rhythm of the music. They took the man's pulse to no avail and asked questions, which my Father and another man tried to answer. No one knew who the man was. He must have come in off the street.

"We'll take him away quietly so as not to disturb the party." And they did, discreetly, deliver him to wherever they take dead bodies. And the party carried on, despite the absence of the now clearly dead man.

And it took only a little time until my Father was once again unmistakably high.

THE CATSKILL MOUNTAINS, 1961. I am eighteen years old, waitressing over winter break to make enough money to continue supporting myself through school. Mother offers me money but Brooklyn College is not that expensive and I need to feel like my own person. The Concord and Grossingers are the most upscale hotels and I have gotten a lucky break and been hired on as an extra at the Concord. The problem with being last hired, besides the two-way disdain between the full-time waitresses and the college kids who invaded them, was that the part-timers got the tables furthest from the kitchen, and last-hired got the tables furthest down the long hall, with the most demanding and worst tipping patrons. At barely over five feet and about a hundred pounds I was no match for the long-legged, heavier, experienced staff that easily passed by me as we trekked back and forth with orders. The food was served on heavy white plates and metal covers kept it warm. They were piled two and sometimes three levels on the tray you carried balanced and raised on your flattened hand and leaned onto your shoulder. Sometimes you stopped briefly on your long walk from the kitchen to your station where you could drop it onto a stand, and balanced your elbow on your hip to stop your arm from trembling, I was certainly one of the slowest waitresses there, which was unappreciated by the people unlucky enough to be seated at one of my tables. My most memorable "guest comment" was from a droll man who, as he placed five dollars in my hand for him and his wife for the weekend, smiled wryly and said: "This is for personality; not for service."

The part-time staff generally had a sense of excitement serving in a vibrant and wealthy environment that we believed we could some day be on the receiving end of, and we took full advantage of our reverse power. We worked hard all day, (if you were quick, a half-hour break between cleaning up breakfast and prepping for lunch, an hour, between lunch and dinner) partied at night on food and alcohol we stole from the kitchen, hardly slept. A lot of the college students worked stoned, but I had not yet tried marijuana, and a half-glass of wine made me unstable.

So this day, overtired and overstressed, as I carried a heavy tray I suddenly felt sharp pains in my head and neck. I thought they would go away, but they persisted, and I started to feel anxious. From nowhere that I could grasp, I suddenly went into panic mode. Why was my head feeling like it was going to explode? I put down the tray and went over to the Maître d' and told him my head was hurting really badly and I couldn't finish serving. I followed him off the floor and by the time we were out of the dining room I had convinced myself that I was having what I now know would be labeled an aneurism. "I need to be taken to the hospital," I told him. "Something's wrong with my head!" And as I said this out loud I knew, I absolutely knew, that I was going to die, that night if I didn't get help. I remember the confused Maître d' finding someone to drive me to the doctor's office, but when we got there several people were in the waiting room and in my mind this was an emergency: no time to wait my turn. Now. I needed help now.

I began to breathe too fast, hyperventilating, and still in my high-collared, form-fitting, white polyester uniform and heavy nylon support stockings I started to feel like I was being strangled. I began to pull off my stockings in the middle of the waiting room, beyond caring what people around me thought or saw. My life depended on it. The receptionist came over to me and I pleaded with her, "Please, please, something is really wrong. Please get me to a hospital."

And I have no memory until I am checked in, close to evening. I remember being in a bed in a dimly lit private room, no longer in a panic because I have convinced myself that there is no stopping this process that has begun, even though my head has stopped pounding. After a nurse checks my vital signs and asks a lot of questions I tell her I know I am dying. Neither she nor the other nurses nor the physician who comes around can convince me otherwise.

Eventually I get a visit from a doctor I find out later is a psychiatrist. I tell him my story, ask him to send for my parents right away so I can see them before I die. He treats me respectfully, agrees to my request, takes down all the information I give him in his notes and when I ask if I can have paper and a pen he returns with a hospital pad and gives me his own fine point blue-ink fountain pen that he takes from his shirt pocket. When he leaves I scrawl out a long letter to my parents, telling them how sorry I am for all the trouble I have inflicted on them over the past eighteen years, and beg them to forgive me. I write how grateful I am for all they've provided, that I should have appreciated it while I could. I ask them to give a couple of my paintings and poems to a friend in Brooklyn and to please take care of themselves. Above all, to never blame themselves; they have done all they could do and I loved them both.

A nurse comes in with a sedative, and I don't want to take it: I am going to die so soon—how can I waste the few hours I have left comatose. "It's orders," she tells me, and though she is nice about it she is firm and explains confidently that it will just be a short rest and I need it for strength.

IT'S LIGHT WHEN I wake up—I have slept ten hours, uninterrupted as far as I can tell. Something doesn't add up. If I am dying, why aren't they monitoring me? And my parents—why didn't they wake me when my parents arrived? They'd be here by now—it was only a three or four hour drive from Brooklyn.

I ring the emergency bell by my bed and in a few minutes a new, more skittish nurse appears. "Have you seen my parents? My mom and dad? The doctor sent for them last night—aren't they here?"

"No one's here, Miss," she answers, looking at me warily. "No visitors waiting for you here."

I ask if I can speak to the doctor who promised he would send for my parents and the nurse picks up the chart at the far end of my bed to find out who it was. "Dr. Miller is who you mean, I think," she says. "He'll be doing rounds in about an hour."

"Please—ask him to come here and talk to me as soon as he gets in," I plead. "I'm so confused. I don't know what's going on."

The thought gets clearer and louder in my head as I wait for the doctor. I now realize that I am not dying. It was a headache, that was all. A commonplace headache. No big deal. Exhaustion. Pain and exhaustion. But now the new thought. How could I have believed I was dying with such certainty? And there it was, on the stand by the bed, the letter, damning evidence that my near-death wasn't a passing suspicion or concern but a belief as concrete as the bed I was lying on. There was only one explanation that made sense. I was crazy. Nuts. Certifiably and completely insane, psychotic like my Father, and I would soon find myself where I had always known I belonged, in a mental hospital, with the other people who couldn't bear living in their environments, who were unable to function in the real world. I close my eyes and try to not think. If I let my mind work it will take me back into the caged wards, electric shock, Haldol, Thorazine, welts on thighs, straightjackets.

And finally he is here, the gentle doctor of the night before, to tell me what I already know: why he has not called my parents. He is here to deliver the diagnosis and that he is packing me up and sending me where? Kings County? Brooklyn State?

I am eighteen now, no longer eligible for Hillside, the holding place for adolescents that Mother almost sent me to three years earlier because I crossed—no, ran over, the line one day—by threatening to burn Mother with the hot iron I was using if she threw the pregnant cat I had brought into the apartment back on the street. It didn't matter that it was simply a ploy, conscious and intended to get her to let me keep the cat. I had scared her and that was that.

The psychiatrist in the stark Hillside interview room staring at me with his huge, black, aggressive eyes in his dark suit, starched shirt and black tie, smugly waiting for me to incriminate myself, feeling myself sink into liquid terror under his gaze, dissociating from any strength or substance I ever had while I answered questions there seemed to be no right answers for.

"Yes," he tells Mother, glad to fill another bed. "Your daughter qualifies for admission."

And it is only because in a conversation Mother has the next day with Dr. Glenn, the one psychiatrist who has ever been understanding and kind to my Father, she tells him her plan to admit me to Hillside, that I am given a reprieve. "She's a teenager," Mother tells me Dr. Glenn said. "They're all a little crazy. Give her time. That's my recommendation. Give her some time."

And now Dr. Miller sits down by the side of my bed and waits for me to talk. "I know what's wrong now," I say. "I understand. I'm not dying. Maybe it's worse. I've had a psychotic break. I've gone crazy."

Dr. Miller doesn't nod his head in agreement as I imagine he will do. He doesn't sadly tell me where I will be sent next. Instead he shakes his head back and forth and offers me a wise and gentle smile. "You're not crazy," he says kindly. "You're just exhausted. And neurotic. Nothing wrong with you some rest and recovery—and maybe some good therapy can't cure."

I don't believe him. I've watched them lie to my Father while they incarcerate him. I know the people in power have no compunction lying to make things easier for themselves. I know what I know.

"You don't believe me, do you?" Dr. Miller correctly reads my mind. "Would it help if you see what I wrote in your chart last night?"

He takes the chart from the foot of the bed, brings it over to me, and turns the page to yesterday. There is his writing in oversize scrawling: Patient is 18y/o/f who came in distraught this eve. dx: psychoneurotic anxiety reaction to stress and exhaustion. rx: rest and recovery, rec. out patient therapy weekly. Discharge TOR tomorrow.

I breathe a sigh of relief, start crying. "Are you saying I'm just scared and overwhelmed? That I'm not crazy?"

"Well, that's what I've been trying to say. Think you're ready to listen now?"

AND THAT FALL, working one weekend at a smaller hotel, I am drawn to Marshall, the tall, thin busboy working at the next station, who has blonde hair and remarkably dark eyebrows, and as I later find out, marshmallow lips, who will become my first lover. We find adjacent rooms in a four-story apartment house with community kitchens and bathrooms that rents rooms to students for $10/week, and after a couple of months, Marshall asks me to go with him to his therapist, under the pretext of helping his therapist help him.

I find myself in an altered state when I enter Mr. Fay's office, a small room at the rear of his several room apartment on the Upper West Side, with his oriental carpet, rocking chair, bookcases, paintings in oil which I find out later he has done, and the light from a long window, a white lace curtain that always seems to have a slight movement, as if blowing in the breeze.

Mr. Fay is fifty-seven years old, a short, Irish redhead, who has huge, wise, blue eyes in his ruddy, expressive, compassionate face. We start talking about how I think Marshall is doing but in no time I have switched to talking about me. When the hour is over I am still talking and Mr. Fay gently asks if I'd like to come back to continue our conversation.

What did I learn from over three years of therapy and intermittent group therapy with Mr. Fay, and occasional returns, which lasted a lot longer than my relationship with Marshall? More than anything, the value, no the necessity, of listening; the healing at the core of being heard and seen and known, and how one can be healed and flourish in a nurturing, accepting relationship, within a safe, loving container. At one point I bring in some poems I have written to Marshall, and I am rewarded by Mr. Fay's eyebrows lifting and his eyes lighting up, his mouth taking me seriously. "You are a good writer," he says, respectfully. "This is important work."

Father, how could it not have been different for you, had you had a caring intervention when you were a child? The unanswered question: how much is chemical? How few people get repaired, cared for, understood, at the cliff edge between sanity and madness.

I DON'T THINK I will ever get used to visiting my Father in the hospital. Not since my first memory of them letting me come inside the building, being led down a dim, long hall with Mother, feeling out of time and waiting in confusion until my Father's defeated, electric-shocked form appeared before me. I never know what to expect. It isn't limited to hospital visits. I don't know what to expect when I arrange to meet him anywhere. Or when he visits me.

I am living next door to Marshall, in our cheap rooming house for students, attending my first year at Brooklyn College. I've made a few friends in the months I have been here and am feeling somewhat stable and almost normal.

On this Saturday morning I am sound asleep when suddenly I hear pounding on my door. "Hey, wake up you lazy bum." And then the raspy refrain: "Wake up, wake up you sleepyhead, wake up, wake up, get out of bed. Is Marshall in there with you? What's happening? Open the door to your lonely old Dad."

Oh my god, I realize as I come to and jolt out of bed. He's high.

"Hi Daddy," I say, giving him a hug, grateful that this is one time Marshall is not in there with me. "What's up?" I glance at my clock and read 5:30 a.m. "Aren't you up a bit early?"

"Times a-wasting, my Little Chickadee," he informs me. His eyes have that glaze I recognize so well and I see he is wearing an old navy blue suit over a white shirt; and the red sneakers he buys when he is in a manic state.

"Interesting shoes," I say.

"You like them?" he responds, smiling proudly.

"No comment," I say, patting him on the back maternally.

"Well, should we get some of these lazy bums up and moving?" he asks me, looking like he's not a day older than seven, even though he is forty-eight years old.

"Let's give 'em a break, Daddy," I tell him. "C'mon, let's go to breakfast. My treat."

"Well, okay," he assents, looking a bit put out for a minute but then back to his childlike innocence. "Where are we going?"

I dress as quickly as possible while he waits outside my room humming loudly, "You've got to get up, got to get up, got to get up in the morning."

Finally I steer him downstairs and we walk to a breakfast place nearby. The rest of the morning and the long day seem like a blur as he talks and talks about his ideas and dreams for a future I now know will never happen. When I was younger, I used to believe his visions and laugh with him and hang on his words. I realize as we walk how far away I am from the trusting child who unconditionally loved her daddy, and I feel a painful knot tighten in my stomach. I'm only eighteen, I think. I shouldn't have to do this.

I am tired by the time we get back to my place in late afternoon. I don't want him to come back with me, but there is no stopping him, unless I get him to put himself in the hospital, and he doesn't seem bad enough yet. And I don't have the stamina to put him in and watch the light go out of his eyes. Maybe I will in a week or two, when I have no choice.

He gets a lot of attention as he energetically climbs the stairs. One of my more uninhibited friends, an artist, is in the hall and he and my Father hit it off at first sight. He thinks my Father is fascinating and they become fast friends. Very fast. Don has a car, my Father finds out, and my Father convinces him to take us for a ride around town. I try to warn Don but he doesn't take me seriously. My dad is charming, the dad Don doesn't have. His father died when he was twelve.

They are children together and I sit in the back seat in amazement, listening to my Father tell Don everything he needs to know to get on in life. Most of the ride is vague but there is no vagueness to the challenge I hear. "I bet you can't keep driving if I spill this Coke over your head." Oh, great, I think, useless in the back seat. Useless, even if I were in the front seat.

"What are you talking about?" Don asks, bewildered but still looking eager to please.

"You heard me," my Father says. "I bet you five bucks you can't keep on driving the car while there's Coke running down your head."

Don laughs. He thinks this is a game. I guess he's right, sort of.

"What do you say, is it a bet?" my Father asks, his face petulant.

"No," Don says. "It's not a bet."

"Chicken," my Father says. "Poor sport, poor sport."

"Leave it alone Daddy," I offer from the back seat.

Don looks confused. "Why would I want to have Coke over my head?" he asks my Father reasonably.

"Why not?" my Father asks and lifts his cup casually over Don's head and I watch stunned as the brown liquid and pieces of broken ice drop down onto Don's thick brown hair and green jacket. Luckily Don keeps control of the car, but I can see in the mirror the liquid running down his face. He is stunned, too, and does not know how to react.

"Put it there," says my Father, who has no such problem. He has dropped his empty cup on the floor and is now extending his hand in a show of brotherly love. "You're a damned good sport."

"Tell you what. I'll take you two out to dinner tonight," my Father says as Don, completely bewildered, tries to concentrate on staying on the road. "There's this fawncy restaurant on the Upper East Side." He emphasizes the high class words. "I'm taking you two 'cause you're such good sports." I feel worn down, from the tension and the constant activity level, but underneath there is a tiny sense of almost exhilaration from the impulsive round of events, the daring of societal mores and values.

Don has had it. My Father is not at all tired. Don declines, saying he has a date and insistently and silently drives us back to 88th Street, and goes his separate way, despite efforts on my Father's side to keep him with us by patting him on the shoulder and telling him to bring his friend along and finally with taunts of "Quitter" and "Boy, you sure had me fooled. I thought you were a good sport."

As for me, I am not sure if I am feeling mortified or not. I am almost inured to these kinds of scenes. But later it goes beyond my immunity system, and I am sure of what I feel.

WE TAKE THE bus to the "fawncy" restaurant and my Father makes a great show of how he's taking his daughter out to dinner and wants the best seat and service in the house. The waiter is gracious enough, ignoring or perhaps not noticing his red sneakers or his glazed eyes. I figure I look passable and perhaps that pulls us through. "What's the best thing you got?" my Father asks the waiter. "Get the most expensive thing on the menu," he says to me. "You're my daughter, so you're worth it." My Father continues to make a spectacle out of himself as the dinner wears on. He has to talk to people at the other tables, to ask the waiter about his personal life, to boast loudly about his ability as a chef and a string of his accomplishments that never happened. Luckily the food turns out to be excellent, and the service, so there isn't anything obvious for him to complain about. The waiter is agreeable, the bread is warm and replenished as soon as the basket empties out, my Father's steak is cooked "almost as good as when I cook it" and there is soft music in the background which he hums to while he's chewing and in-between his comments. After a while I almost find myself relaxing. Maybe I can at least have a little bit of peace. Dessert is an extravaganza of pastry with berries and syrups and is blessedly uneventful.

It's not until the waiter puts the check down in front of my Father that I begin to go back to my normal vigilant state. There's something about the way my Father is looking at the bill that alerts me but I don't get what it is at first. "How about you pay now and I'll pay you back tomorrow?" my Father asks, grinning calmly. The bill is for almost fifteen dollars. My rent for the week is ten dollars and I live on only seventy a month. In my purse is about three dollars.

"What do you mean, Daddy? How am I supposed to pay? I spent my last few dollars on rent."

"Well, I guess we wash dishes," my Father says, disgusted with me.

"You're joking," I say. "You have a job. You must have money."

"Okay. I'm joking," he returns. "But if you can't pay I don't know how we're going to get out of here."

I am angry not with him but at myself. I should have known better. I should have checked to make sure he had money on him before we left. I shouldn't be here now. I should have my head examined for letting myself get into a situation like this. Why hadn't I checked to see if he had money before we came here? I should have known better. I can't believe how stupid I am. But wait. Maybe he is just putting me on.

Obviously many steps ahead of me and reading my mind my Father assures me that he doesn't have any money. "Nothing," he says, pointing to his suit pockets. "Search me if you like. C'mon, search me if you don't believe me. You'll see. Jesus what do you need to do to get someone to believe you?"

I choose not to respond to the irony of his last statement. Instead I try to figure out if there is any way at all out of this new nightmare.

I pick up the check on the little brown dish and we gather ourselves up and walk over to the register. The manager is waiting. My hands trembling and my heart racing I tell him in a whisper that we have a problem. My Father forgot his wallet. All I have is three dollars.

The man looks at us as if he had smelled a rat all along and now here it was under his nose and he was not about to let it go. "You mean after all this you can't pay for your dinner?" he asks loudly enough to attract attention.

"Hey, don't make it into a big deal," yells my Father, stepping in front of me, his temper activating in quick stages. "We'll wash your crummy dishes for you if you want us to. That should pay for the few bucks your food costs you. The mark-ups in these places is ninety percent that's what it is. Ninety percent. And you're just a two-bit cashier so don't act so hoity-toity with us."

Now I can really feel myself shaking. "Let it go, please," I tell the angry but bewildered man. "I'll send a check in the mail tonight, and it'll cover the costs. I promise I will." I try to catch his eyes behind my Father's head and I do what I hate to do, it grinds my stomach to do, but I do anyway. I point my finger to my head, make circles around my ear, and point to my Father. "He's nuts," I outline with my lips, and between the words and the crazy sign he puts the evening together and decides it's better to back off.

"She will too," my Father vouches for me as I write down the name and address of the restaurant on a napkin. "She's good for her word."

And so we are allowed to leave the restaurant. I start to breathe again with relief, my Father in a mellow if not euphoric mood. "Not a bad dinner," he says. "For the price."

I wonder again what's real and what's not real. The phrase comes to my mind. Yeah he's crazy all right. Crazy, like a fox. I have to shake myself to remember that my Father when he is "normal" doesn't do things like this. He just doesn't.

When I finally extricate myself from my Father and make my way home I am shocked at how exhausted I am. That night, in bed with Marshall, I find myself sobbing from deep inside my center and feel a burning hate for a universe that allows so much insanity.

MY FATHER CONTINUES to come over any time, day or night, to talk, just be around, joke, argue. Always explosive with energy, dressed in the same costume: old navy-blue suit, shirt unpressed, telltale red tennis shoes.

I am supposed to be studying for exams while all this is going on. A friend studies with me, history, history. It all seems irrelevant. What does it mean in the context of life? Pages of text to be memorized regardless of their authenticity. So many gaps and biases, so much unreality in the frozen, censored world of books. Memorize it anyway. Give them what they want and they will give you what you want. That was the only way to remain in the stream of normality.

The day I convinced my Father to sign himself into the hospital I dressed carefully and waited for him. He came in an old black car he'd acquired that hardly ran. He came on time, so I let some of the anxiety escape and began to feel calmer. I went over to the car and began to get in.

"Wait," my Father said. "I was just thinking. If I've got to go into Brooklyn State I'm sure I'm not competent to drive a car."

How is it that he was still capable of such shock effects after all those years?

"I don't understand. How are you going to go if you don't drive? I guess we could take the train and the bus but that will take hours."

"I'm not taking the train or the bus," he said. I said nothing.

"I'll only go in if _you_ drive," my Father told me, absolutely and petulantly, like a child who has compromised to the extreme limit of his capacity.

"Daddy, you know I can't drive," I told him. "How could I take you there in traffic and everything, all the way to Brooklyn?"

"I'll help you," he said nonchalantly. "That's my last offer: take it or leave it."

"I don't have a driver's license," I said, feeling I was talking for nothing.

"So who needs a license?" he responded.

At least he was in a good mood. I knew that might not last long and at the moment I didn't care much more than he did if I had a license, and I had a little experience driving around the block in a friend's car a few times, not to mention pretend driving with my Father since before I could reach the pedals. Driving from the Upper West Side of Manhattan to Brooklyn, with just my Father for driver's instructor with his erratic behavior, however, wasn't in the same category as driving around a block, pretend driving, or having a license.

"All right," I said. "Let's try it."

Strangely enough the ride was fairly smooth. I managed, with his very competent direction, "First—now second—turn to the left—watch out—" to get over the bridge and into Brooklyn. In fact, the ride was so smooth my Father thought he ought to put some excitement into it and as we slowed down a couple of times he decided to test out my skills by turning off the ignition and making me start up again—without any coaching. Somehow we arrived at the hospital without any tickets or accidents and my Father appeared to be quite proud both of me for my driving and of himself for his idea and his direction.

"Let's try that again, sometime," he quipped in a jovial mood as we walked up the steps of the main building. I felt emotionally and physically drained of all energy, and yet I knew if I showed it he would never go through with this.

"Why not?" I answered.

Still in a good mood my Father asked to see the doctor on duty who it turned out knew him well from before.

"What can we do for you, Mr. Levy?" he asked.

"Well, it's my daughter, Doctor," he said. "She wants me to sign myself in for a while."

"What about you?"

"Sure," he said. "Whatever my daughter says."

And in a little while my Father signed the papers on the cluttered metal desk giving up his rights to remain free. And I watched them take off his watch and his wallet, and give them to me. I kissed him goodbye and he smiled and winked at me. They took him up to the ward, and the next time I saw my Father, he was sedated and dressed in wrinkled white.

MAG

Your history.
Do your history.
But my Father's mad.
But we're going to die.
But my Father's mad
But we're going to
No matter.
Your history.
Do your history.

But he's mad going to die
Do your history
Madgoingto
Histry
madgoing
histry
magodie
doyorisry
mag
Uhhhhhhhhhhhhhhhhhhooooooooooooooohhhhhhhhhhhh

A N ARTICLE IN *Psychology Today* finds in a study of severely depressed women that they all had four things in common, none of which was a family history of depression. First, they had all lost a parent before they reached age eleven. Second, they were at home without outside jobs. Third, they had at least three children living at home (the only category which my Father did not fit into, but then he was a man at home in non-liberated times and had lost both parents). And fourth, all were married to people they could not communicate with.

I am twenty-one years old, and because there is a shortage of teachers I have received, with many other recent graduates, an emergency teaching credential. I am hired as a second-grade classroom teacher at PS 122 in Manhattan, even though my bachelor's degree is in the unrelated field of creative writing.

My Father has been admitted to Brooklyn State, again, and I arrive at the hospital as quickly as I can. His best and only friend, Danny, is there.

My Father is very high and seems to be bursting under terrific intensity and strain; he has clearly not yet been given any medication.

Suddenly as he rambles on there is a moment of silence, as he seems struck by a profound, novel thought. Then, in a hoarse, burning voice, his eyes glaring, he demands of us: "What am I, anyway—a genius or an idiot?"

I feel my stomach spinning, head pounding. I have no answer for him and the cruel, dull emptiness reverberates in my ears.

Then, the clear, reasoned words come from Danny, who is looking at my Father calmly and with affection.

"You're not either, Sam. Not a genius, not an idiot. You're just a human being like the rest of us."

And then—how could I believe my eyes?

They call it chemistry, but how can chemistry account for the feverishness evaporating from my Father's face, for his eyes losing their thick glaze, for his body dropping its rigidity? Even more vital, how can chemistry account for his release from the hospital in one week, without intervention, no electric shock, no medications, instead of the usual several-month period? How does chemistry account for the predictable depressive cycle never following at all?

These are not idle questions. We are invested in these answers, my Father and I.

DURING THE PAST five years I have taught second and third grade classes and remedial reading in the New York public school system, while slowly completing the required classes for a master's degree in literature in the evenings. Allan has been my steady boyfriend all this time and this year I have been hired as a school social worker in Connecticut, even though I have no counseling credentials, because the principal incorrectly believed I would be easy to order around.

I take the bus into the city every other week to see Allan and to meet my Father on Sundays for lunch. My Father doesn't have many connections. Aunt Ruth is sick a lot and Danny is involved in his own life. Mother severed her ties to my Father several years ago, even before going through with the divorce—in actuality an annulment on grounds of insanity, that she obtained without needing his signature while he was in Brooklyn State.

My Father's face, the eyebrows so wonderfully shaped strained down in pain and non-hope. His mouth with never a smile or word. His posture bent and heavy. In the hospital—did he really go in without letting me know?

I waited, waited for him at the corner as I had done for these last months. But my Father did not come. At his rooming house the man who took the rent said he had left and he did not know where he had gone. "Did he leave any address—any way to contact him?" I asked. "No," the man said, "but he left a valise. It's down here if you want to look at it."

In the valise, old torn newspapers and dirty underwear, a broken transistor radio, Kleenex, used and unused, napkins, old notes which seemed meaningless, a broken clock and some rags.

"Where is my Father?" I ask again and the man repeats that he does not know. Finally I leave and go into a drug store, call all the mental hospitals I can think of and ask if my Father has come. "No," they say, "There is no one of that description here."

I go back to the rooming house. "Mister, I am going to have to go to the police to find out where my Father is."

"Wait," he says, "I think I might have a lead."

My Father had been getting tired a lot, he said, and came out less and less in the last two weeks. He had tried to help him out, even asked if he needed money or food or what was wrong. My Father had shaken his head and walked on, hardly seeming to hear him. When my Father said he was leaving he had asked where he was going and he'd said to a hospital and when he asked which one he had said the one down the street, which turned out to be the Catholic hospital.

It was not very far and I walked down, leaving the valise. I asked at the desk if a Sam Levy was there and what was wrong and they seemed pleased to see me. He had said he had no relatives. They didn't know what was wrong with him except he was malnourished and dehydrated, probably alcoholic. I explained that my Father didn't drink, didn't like the taste, even of beer. The doctor—I guess the resident—gave me a skeptical look and said that relatives didn't generally know what went on with alcoholics. I was furious but tried to keep my temper. So righteous he was, so sure he knew what he knew. So, for whatever that joke is worth my Father is still on their register—the only hospital that has him labeled as an alcoholic, main symptoms presented and diagnosed, because he had stopped eating and drinking and tested dehydrated.

I did not recognize my Father. I had thought I had seen him in all states, but this was surely the worst: He was so still, and had not shaved for days, he just lay in the bed in hospital clothing, looking dried up and wrinkled, when he was still only in his fifties and ordinarily had few lines on his face. A nurse's aide was approaching his bed with food on a tray and I stopped her and asked about my Father who was sound asleep. She took me to the side, and whispered that he was still almost all of the time, that he would not get up to eat or shave, that he said he could not raise his hands, though there was no medical reason for this, she had been told.

"How is he eating, then?" I asked, not wanting to know.

"I feed him by hand," she answered. "If I did not he would not eat."

I felt my legs trembling with fear and rage, fear of how far my Father was going and rage at his lack of will to live. I went to the bed and shook my Father until he woke and looked at me in a dream. "Get up," I said, "your supper is here and you had better eat."

"I can't," he whispered to me, "I can't lift my hands."

"Like hell you can't," I answered him in terror, and threw off the top of his sheet and began to help him up. The nurse came with the tray and placed it by the bed.

"I can't," he said again, and the nurse shook her head to show she understood. I pulled my Father again and he finally sat up. I put the spoon roughly in his hand.

"Start," I ordered, afraid if I did not I would cry or scream and too that he would not listen to me. He met my eyes then, and began to say I can't, but looking at me he seemed to know he was lying, and lowered his lids. He lifted his hand and put the spoon into the mashed potatoes soggy with margarine and water. To the shock of the nurse and himself, and by this time me, my Father began to eat.

M Y FATHER WAS so much better when I left to go back to work in Connecticut. In only a few hours he had shaved, with some help, and he was sitting up in bed looking at a newspaper. And the week after when I returned he was in a chair watching television instead of lying semi-comatose in bed.

If they had not moved him then, perhaps he would have been all right for some while, but the doctor decided he did not belong in the ward with the physically ill and transferred him to the small cramped quarters of the mentally ill in one of the wings. And decided to give him Elavil, a drug which it turned out he was allergic to.

When I returned the week after, my Father was gone, and my thoughts scattered. I was enraged, thinking he had left without regard for where he would go or what he would do. But no, he had been transferred, the nurse told me. They wanted to send him to another hospital, but meanwhile felt it best to keep him on the mental ward—though she thought he "weren't no trouble here at all."

There were three beds in the small room. In one was a man about my Father's age who kept talking about the cruelty of the world and how they would not let him leave though he was perfectly all right, and in the other an older man who was in a constant debate with the first man about whose children cared about them most, each challenging the other with, "If your children care so much, how come they never come to visit?"

My Father was in the third bed, in the corner by the barred window. I walked over to him amid greetings from the other two patients. "He won't talk to you," the older man said. "He ain't talked since he got here." I looked at my Father's face, which was again strained and old as it had been, all the work of the past month nullified. I called to him, touched his thin shoulder, but he did not answer. I began to shake him, but he did not move. His breathing seemed so slow, I could scarcely be sure he was alive. Finally, I began to lightly slap his face and call louder. Still my Father did not move or open his eyes. I began to panic and left the room to stop the hysteria from immobilizing me. There was no one on the floor to talk to, and from what I had seen of nurses and attendants as well as psychiatrists, I wasn't hopeful of any answers from them anyway.

In a few minutes I went back and this time did not try to be gentle. "Daddy," I called out close to his face and pinched him hard on his shoulders. He grunted and then he opened his silver-blue eyes wide and saw me. He smiled at me, the most frightening smile I have ever seen. His eyes stared, and his lips were tight and hard. His teeth showed in an almost demonic grin, not moving, grating at me in what seemed diabolical hatred and hysteria together. Just for a moment my Father smiled this smile of horror. He closed his eyes, turned his head and returned to sleep.

I went to the desk and rang the bell over and over until a nurse appeared. She was not unfriendly and seemed busy rather than brusque. I told her who I was and that I wanted to know what had happened to my Father in one short week. She hesitated, then said she did not know exactly what was wrong—just that he seemed so stubborn. Wouldn't eat or speak or drink—in fact, she said, lowering her voice, he wouldn't even go to the bathroom, which she thought was really obstinate and peculiar.

"Wouldn't go to the bathroom?" I asked. "For how long?" Well, she wasn't sure. A couple of days, at least, it seemed to her. "Would you come in with me to see him?" I asked her. "I have never seen him like this. Something is wrong. I know it is." We went back in and I asked her to check my Father again. She checked his stomach. "Why my Lord," she said, "it's about as hard as a rock."

"Where's the doctor on this ward?" I asked, trying to keep control of my nerves.

"Well . . . it's not his hours . . ."

"I don't care about his hours. My Father is sick. I want the doctor now."

She called him in finally. It was an emergency, she thought, and he finally came over.

"His stomach is distended," I told the doctor. "What kind of medication is he on?"

He came to my Father's bed and raised the sheets over his still body. "Yes," he said, "there is something seriously wrong. I will get a catheter and clear this up. It looks like if I don't his bladder will burst."

Well, this woke my Father up. I waited outside the room as the doctor put the catheter up his urinary tract and I listened to my Father scream and scream and scream. As my grandfather had screamed as he lay dying of cancer, screaming for them to take out the pacemaker which tortured him so and to let him have peace and die, so my Father screamed for the doctor to let him alone and stop pushing that tube into his body with no sedatives or anesthetic.

And yet when he was through my Father was once again alive, and with some small grip on this world again. He knew me and tired though he was, his eyes were open and he no longer smiled that bizarre, demonic smile.

FINALLY, MY FATHER was transferred to Kings County, the holding place for patients before they are placed in a State Hospital from a medical facility. He was to go to Rockland State, they said, far out in the country, because of the zoning system. It would be very difficult to visit him and I was afraid of what would happen to him alone most of the time in an unfamiliar place. At least at Brooklyn State people knew him and he eventually was released with at least some fragment of himself left. And it had become a kind of home to him, too. Between transient hotel rooms, Brooklyn State seemed permanent and always available.

I went from one place and person to another trying to convince them not to send my Father to Rockland State, pleading hardship of travel for his sister, his only visitor outside of me and Danny, explaining as well as I could, but to no avail. Finally, we went the underground way and my Aunt Ruth said my Father lived at her address. Discouraging, that legitimate reasons will not work in the bureaucratic red-tape system, and that a technical lie will open a series of doors.

Kings County in the sixties has to have been the filthiest of institutions. There were scores of mummified-looking people sitting on the sides on benches or pacing in the wards, all wearing faded blue cotton robe-pajamas and slippers without backs without socks underneath. Visitors, not many, went over to their own as the doors allowed entrance. It was the first time I'd been to Kings County Mental Ward, and so I was shocked to see every once in a while running across the floor, all but on the ankles of patients, little brown mice, scurrying after crumbs and each other from bench to bench amid the dust and dirt. My Father was standing up when I came, which was better than I'd seen him in a long time, and after embracing I asked him what about the mice. He shrugged and didn't seem to mind, and neither did anyone else, so I tried to ignore them, glad that at least I was not barefoot.

We had a good talk and my Father seemed glad that he would be going to Brooklyn State and not Rockland. Then we sat together by the window quietly till the attendant told everyone to leave, as visiting was over.

He seemed to improve steadily. The next week when I came in from Connecticut my Father was in Brooklyn State, and had been placed on the ground floor, in their new program of no locks, no keys on all but the 4th floor which held the violent, suicidal, and runaways. He was wearing a regular shirt and pants, and he had shaved, and the people on the ward did not look very disturbed or very hopeless. I was so glad to see him like that; I had thought for weeks that hope was pointless. When I went to the desk the attendant said my Father could go out for the day, without my even having to sign him out, and that the only restriction was that he had to be in by eight o'clock. We went for a long walk, up the hill to the park benches at the top of the street cluttered with buses and cars and people, milling our way through the crowds. When we finally got to the parkway we found a newspaper and shared it, reading under a tree while traffic shot by. There did not seem to be much to say, but my Father seemed much more relaxed and out of the despair he had been in. We ate dinner in a small restaurant and about seven o'clock I left to return home. And weeks passed like this, precious weeks passed, uneventfully, before things began to change.

THE LAST TIME I saw my Father began as just another ordinary day. I parked outside the hospital and went up the elevator to the fourth floor where my Father was now. In the elevator with me was a short fat woman about fifty years old who began to talk. "I am feeling so good now," she told me. "So good." Yet I noticed that her eyes had no expression in them and she did not smile as she said this. "A while ago I got a lobotomy, and it changed my life." She spoke so slowly, so mechanically, as if she were reciting a lesson she had learned well but was still cautious about not forgetting a crucial word or phrase. "I am feeling so good," she repeated, looking at me now and with a frozen despair covering her eyes and face.

I shivered in nausea as I got out and went to the locked men's ward where my Father was. I knocked on the door and finally the guard saw me and came over with his key. As he opened the door a muscular, unshaven man flew over to me and began to yell that he was going to destroy me and all those like me. I backed away and the guard ordered him to go back to the other side of the ward, which he did, suddenly meek. I remembered the time I came to see my Father and he told me of how cruelly the guards were treating him and I did not believe him as he was high and beside himself with anger. Then my Father had pulled down his pants and showed me on his thigh two-inch wide welts going across him, swelled up and red-brown. "Look what they did to me," he said. "Now do you believe me?" And I, in impotence and stupidity, stood there knowing not at all what to do, being only sixteen and unable to sort out justice or injustice, pain and hatred, with a removed part of me thinking but of course not saying, you probably asked for it.

I finally got in and stood by the desk, and got the papers to sign my Father out for the day. He had been on this ward now for the past month, because several times instead of coming back at eight p.m. he had stayed out overnight and come back in the morning. It wasn't as if he was running away—he kept coming back. But to be allowed on the open ward he had to obey this rule, which he didn't even seem to comprehend. Consequently, he had to stay on the locked ward all week and could not go to the restaurant down the corner or even the grounds to rest under a tree or for walks down to the stores.

It was early October and still warm in New York, and inside the hospital the heat and closeness seemed unbearable. I could not understand why my Father had persisted in staying out overnight knowing that he would be taken up to the maximum security ward. He was not like the other people up there, the hard-core criminals, catatonic backward patients or serious runaways. I spoke with him about this and told him that if he would be careful about getting back at the right time I would talk to the guards about letting him downstairs again, but my Father looked at me kind of puzzled, then, avoiding my eyes asked me what for? I explained about the different types of people on the fourth floor ward, about not being able to go out. I told him all the obvious things he could see for himself, but my Father just shrugged and said, "It's all the same. It's the same to me up there as downstairs. It's all a nuthouse anyway." And so I had his answer, and asked no more questions.

On this day, as we drove through Brooklyn heading toward Coney Island, I didn't say anything to my Father about changing wards. We listened to the radio in the car and even hummed along with some of the songs. He seemed to be in a good mood and even joked with me some. At Coney Island we walked on the boardwalk, snacked and watched as people played various games in the small booths. We played skeeball as we often did, visited the auctions, watched the passersby.

As we walked off the boardwalk onto the side streets my Father picked up a large stick, almost a cane, he had found among the garbage. Almost as if he were high he began to fool around with it, pretending he was a cripple, twirling it, acting as a child or a free spirit might. I felt somewhat embarrassed for it reminded me of all the times his free spirit got out of control, and he seemed to pick up on my hesitation. "Are you embarrassed by me?" he asked. Ashamed, I admitted that yes just a little, I was. My Father surprised me by smiling apologetically and putting the stick down. I linked my arm through his and we walked on.

Somehow we began talking about my plans for the summer, when my contract at the school in Connecticut was over. Surprised at myself, I mumbled something about places one could go, things that might be elsewhere. "If I didn't have commitments here, I might go to California," I said, laughing, but not really joking. A friend planned to move there in the summer, and had invited me to come with her. My relationship with Allan wasn't going anywhere. California seemed so attractive, a place far from the past, the symbiotic ties, the unhappiness and disappointments. California seemed far enough away to start a new life.

Did what I say affect my Father? Did he hear the meaning behind what I tried to say and not say?

I wonder now if I would have been free to go to California as I did if my Father had not done his part. Would I have felt that I had to stay? I never had to make that choice: he made it for me.

That evening, when I drove us back to the hospital, there were no parking spaces available. I double-parked and prepared to walk my Father to the desk and sign him in. As I started to get out of the car, my Father said decisively, "I'll go in by myself."

"I don't mind," I answered, beginning to get out of the car anyway.

"What's the matter," my Father asked, his voice challenging and childish at the same time, "Don't you trust me?"

What should a daughter do if her father asks her to trust him? As I hesitated, not wanting to upset him, my Father opened his car door, walked down the street and up to the front door and waved me goodbye. He stood there, waving me off, until I finally drove away.

What should I have said to my Father? What should I have done? He was in the locked ward because he had left the hospital without permission, so how could I possibly trust him? Still, he always came back, so I did trust that he would return.

I never suspected that he would disappear from sight, would make no contact with anyone for all these years, or no, I would not have let him go without signing him back in myself. Or would I have?

Who knows how my Father's life has been all this time? Perhaps this was the best thing he could have done, for himself and even for me. He escaped. He exercised his own will, and part of me is glad that he did. Yet I mourn, too, for my Father, gone without a trace, and I cannot even know if he is alive or dead.

PART TWO

GONE

"Can't Get Used To Losing You, No Matter What I Try To Do."

MONTHS OF MISERABLE hours checking morgues, hospitals, prisons and cheap motels that house transients and frightening hours driving and walking up and down the seedy streets of Manhattan give me no information and no Father.

I am starving for normalcy, and yearn for a family of my own to create on a consistent basis the rare moments of warmth and connection I experienced as a child. My almost six-year relationship with Allan is still stalled and neither of us is willing to commit to the other and, without any obligations to my Father to hold me back, soon after the end of the school year I pack up my few belongings, load them into an old Chevy and leave New York to find a new life 3,000 miles away.

One month after arriving, I meet Robert, also a transplant from the East Coast, at a singles' event at the Unitarian Church in Berkeley. Robert is almost a decade older than I am, and, having broken two engagements, is now almost ready to get married. In my mind, he has sanely passed the threshold age of thirty-three when my Father was labeled manic-depressive, a diagnosis believed to surface in one's early thirties.

Robert and I are kindred, creative spirits. We have the same music collections, poems, and art reproductions. Our rare records of *The Ballet of The Red Shoes* becomes a tie that unites us through the years. We make love well and although we argue we are hopeful that we can work things out. Robert teaches me places I have never known. I go from the chaotic crowds of Times Square to the rugged beauty of the Mendocino Coast where timeless, breathtaking sunsets reflected on a vast ocean affect me far more than the fireworks on the beach at Coney Island or the lights of Broadway ever have. Most Saturdays we pack up our paints and Robert drives us to one of his cherished places and we find a place to rest and set up our simple materials. He introduces me to Yosemite's waterfalls, Lodi's historic town, the beaches of Santa Cruz, the culture, restaurants and museums of San Francisco, and Berkeley's hippie streets and hidden outposts.

Robert's mother has died three years earlier of cancer. His father has moved into a mobile home park in Florida, and visits us soon after we become involved. In contrast to my Father with his see-saw moods, Claude Smith is a stable, predictable man, more of a polished stone than a rock. His nickname is Smitty, and with his upside down flower pot hat and thick glasses, incontrovertible sanity, and easy-going southern manners, he becomes a stand-in for my Father. I am more drawn to him than I am to Robert, my introspective, moody, angular, poet lover, soon to become my husband. Claude takes to me immediately, nicknames me for no reason JR for jack rabbit and I become his sidekick. This is as close as I have been to the role I was in with my Father, when his highs were fun and exciting, before they went spinning out of control.

After eight months, Robert and I are married in the Unitarian Church in Davis, California, without my Father to give me away, so we don't include the walk down the aisle. Our ceremony is simple and informal, written by us with a fragile hope for the future. We exchange the intricate gold rings we have had made for us in the gold country, with the diamond from Robert's mother's engagement ring placed in the setting made for me. Robert has had engraved inside my ring: *Alpha-Omega* and I have had inscribed in his: *I Love Thee*. We find a border collie mix puppy at the pound and name her Snoodles, a combination of the names of the dogs we had in childhood—Robert's dog, Snoopy and mine, Cuddles—and feel like we are a family. Robert becomes comfortable and at home as a reference librarian at Sierra College in Rocklin, and I am accepted into the master's program at the School of Social Work, Sacramento. After two years, we buy a brick and stucco two-story house in Sacramento and even plant a vegetable garden and plum and peach trees.

Our life isn't perfect, but it is more than I have ever had. Mother and Robert's father Claude visit every few months, but my Father, become background noise, is still missing.

I KNOW HOW my Father and Mother met only from her point of view. The meeting place, in Brooklyn, is a dance hall with an area for shooting pool in an adjoining room. Mother, twenty-five, is there for the evening dance with her friends; my Father, twenty-three, is alone, there to hang around, shoot some pool. Mother has on a new velvet green dress with a green wide satin bow, that ties in back, princess style. Her hair is permanented, soft brown and shoulder length, and her naiveté and seriousness are appealing. She is small, only five feet, and very popular at the dance. My Father is not dressed up at all.

Perhaps it was simply chance that my Father looked up from a game, saw Mother and impulsively crossed the line into the dance hall to ask her to dance with him. She consented, although she says she was not interested in him but did not know how to refuse. She gave him her phone number, for the same reason, but went home with someone else. Mother says my Father called her several times until he finally succeeded in getting her to go out with him. His humor and childlike qualities were endearing as were his earthy manner and style. She felt at ease with him even on their first date, she tells me, and this was unusual, as she generally felt uncomfortable around men.

One of the conversations that took place between them seems very important to Mother. After he told her his age, she refused to tell him how old she was, being almost two years older at twenty-five and said enigmatically, "I age like the years." Unruffled by this, he sent her a Valentine's card on Feb.14, 1939 to which he had added the lines:

> Lillian, dear, will you be mine,
> Even though you're thirty-nine?

For whatever the reason, this was the relationship that lasted. After two years of dating they were married, hardly knowing each other despite the long courtship, not even vaguely discerning what could follow, though friends warned Mother against marrying someone as uneducated, unstructured, and financially unstable as my Father, and her parents were appalled by Mother's decision. No one considered what might happen to my Father.

M Y FATHER WAS the youngest of four children, ten to twenty-three years old, when his mother died undergoing emergency gall bladder surgery, just a year after his father succumbed to cancer. According to Aunt Ruth, my Father was their mother's brightest child, her favorite. "When they lowered Mother into the grave, your father became hysterical. He tried to throw himself into the grave with her, crying, 'I don't want to live anymore.' Herbie and me had to hold him back forcibly. Finally, he fell into my arms, sobbing."

Is it strange for a ten-year-old child, twice bereaved, to want to give up and die himself? Is it a sign of mental illness to come or is it a precipitating cause of emotional instability? Studies have shown that incidents of depression are highest in those who have lost a parent by age eleven; my Father lost both his parents before that fragile age.

What happens to a child, my Father, orphaned? His brothers, Herbie and Joe, seventeen and fourteen, are old enough to find an apartment together. Aunt Ruth, married with a newborn child, offers to take my Father in and her husband, Will, allows him to live with them only because he receives seven dollars a week from ADC, Aid to Dependent Children, for doing so.

Will makes no secret of resenting my Father, so he stays away as much as he can when Will is home. Life is simpler if you keep out of sight and trouble most of the time, and fall asleep at night in the kitchen on blankets near the stove, so my Father stays mostly invisible. After school he babysits his niece, who will in the future describe him as "my protector, wherever I went, always gentle with me."

My Father was famous in his neighborhood as a child prodigy. From the time he was six, he could add up several 3-digit numbers in his head in a few seconds. Aunt Ruth tells me, "Sammy would say to anyone, 'Ask me, go on, ask me to add up some numbers and I bet you a penny I get it right.'" He could add them up a lot faster than the person he'd challenged to challenge him, who would be slowly adding up the numbers on paper to see if my Father's answers were correct.

Later my Father would charge a nickel to add up columns of figures, and after a while he wouldn't do it for less than a dime, and made a good amount of money which he cheerfully shared with the rest of the neighborhood. But despite his abilities, he dropped out of school to work at odd jobs and help with the bills when he was just fourteen. He never thought of it as a great loss, since he didn't fit in at school, anyway.

Mother told me that when she first met my Father he would challenge her, the college graduate and accountant, to ask him a math problem and he would astound her by giving her an answer in a flash. At first she thought he must be making wild guesses but after her calculations she'd find out that he was invariably correct. My Father could never explain how he knew the answers; he just did. No wonder he couldn't fit into the school system. Teachers required you to show your work and he couldn't show anything but the result. Perhaps if he had had parents and support and wasn't half-living on the streets it would have made a difference and his formal education wouldn't have ended so abruptly, so soon.

The story was that my Father had a perfect ear for music. Mother told me that once, at a Benny Goodman concert in the park, my Father told her that a note was off in one of the pieces and when they went over and asked Benny Goodman he said that my Father was correct—he had heard the wrong note as well.

My Father and his brothers were a trio that crooned in their raspy voices around their neighborhoods for fun. They never played any instruments though. No one picked up an old guitar or drum set and experimented.

My Father may have had a great ear for music, but, as he knew, his vocal tone wasn't appealing, and he wanted me to learn to sing the songs he loved. He taught me "Mammy," "A Bicycle Built For Two," "Take Me Out to The Ball Game" and my parents' song "Begin The Beguine." When we came home from seeing new musicals as they were released in the theaters, I got lesson after lesson on singing show tunes like "It Might As Well Be Spring," "If I Loved You" and "Can't Help Lovin' Dat Man."

And when my Father came home with the first black and white TV on our block—generating my one short-lived stint of popularity, since Mother allowed a few neighbor children to sit quietly and watch with us—I learned the songs that made it to the top of the Hit Parade. My Father was my critic and trainer for "Mr. Sandman," "Unchained Melody" and "Love Is A Many Splendored Thing," which I never got on pitch. I worked on the songs whole-heartedly, thrilled and honored to have my Father spend so much time with me.

I T IS HARDER to remember these good moments with my Father than the months of turmoil. In between breakdowns there was a respite of two or even three years before my Father again lost control, was shocked or drugged into compliance and went through a slow recovery at home. I would find him asleep on his side on the maroon couch when I came in from school, and be careful not to disturb him until in a few weeks he would come around and again be my in-between-breakdowns Father: gentle, patient, good humored, and generous, the one person who could always wash away my sadness with a joke and the backs of his fingers lovingly and slowly brushing across my cheek.

Mother is the one who was impatient, volatile and hard to live with. Mother grew up in Poland during the pograms, and had to hide under the bed in terror when the soldiers broke in the door of her family's flat. She and her mother hid in a farmer's hay wagon when she was seven to get out of Poland and escaped by boat to England, where her father had found work as a journalist earlier, and two years later they all arrived in the United States.

The chaos that came with my Father's breakdowns was anathema to Mother, who desperately needed calm and stability, and clearly married the wrong person to attain them. Mother was usually too anxious to appreciate what she did have, even the moments of lightness when nothing visible was wrong.

A SONG PLAYS on the radio and brings my Father back. We used to walk for hours on Times Square and listen to music blasting from adjacent stores, each with its own station or recording turned up to top volume in order to attract people wandering the hot streets. We would walk slowly, stopping every once in a while to look at records or cameras or luncheon specials or whatever caught our attention.

One day my Father paused at a home goods store and we stood inside the doorway, listening to the song playing. My Father, stuttering slightly just coming out of depression, asked me if I knew the song. I listened closely to the words "Can't get used to losing you/No matter what I try to do/ Gonna spend my whole life through/Loving you." I could see my Father's pain and also his relief at someone, the writer of the song, understanding and expressing his emotions for him. I wanted to tell my Father that I undersood what he was going through and I hoped my eyes revealed what I could not say in words.

The same song playing now brings it all back. I am drawn into my Father's hopelessness and loneliness. "Can't get used to losing you," meant of course for Mother, but perhaps it goes further back, to my Father's mother, dead before he had a chance to process mourning, bereavement, despair.

And now it fits for me, too, having lost not my mother, but my Father.

LAST NIGHT, THINKING of my Father on his fifty-eighth birthday, New Year's Eve. I wonder what he is doing, alone in New York, the city of anonymity and dreams. I fantasize he is in torn clothing, not warm enough, lonely, walking on Broadway or among the crowds waiting for the falling of the glossy ball at the stroke of midnight on Times Square, 1972, 1973. His silver-blue eyes are strained and lost in black circled shadows, his mouth thinning, without humor or hope, walking alone along the streets of the city. Perhaps he is again in a room at a cheap hotel, dirty and unshaven, torn newspapers over the floor with dirty underwear underneath, soiled sheets and the smells of non-caring; or maybe he is closed up in a ward with other lost people, wandering the halls like zombies, taking as home a place where there is nothing expected or given to you. I wonder if my Father is even alive.

I do not want to think of my Father. I am here safe and stable, happily married, for the first time living in a home of my own, and taking classes in social work at California State University, Sacramento, hoping to help people like my Father and me and do some good in the world. And most exciting, we are having our first child. Life is peaceful as it never has been for me before, and I hate that my Father haunts me with his grief and despair.

IT HAS TAKEN us more than a year to get pregnant and, now that I finally am, the nausea, swelling, and even the Braxton Hicks contractions in my eighth month amount to just minor inconveniences. I devour the book *A Child Is Born* with its wonderful photos of babies in utero, especially the three-month-old walnut size curled-up fetus and the fully formed six-month-old with its thumb comfortably in its delicate mouth.

It is an era of natural childbirth and Lamaze classes have us well prepared for a straight-forward birth. So we are confident and excited when contractions are strong and close together in the middle of the night and we are reasonably calm while Robert drives us to the hospital twenty minutes from our home.

Just as Robert pulls up to the parking lot, my water breaks and spills down my legs and I excitedly put my hand down to feel it. In the bright artificial lights I see that there is not clear but red bloody liquid all over me, my clothing and the car. I am in a fog as Robert lifts me into a wheelchair and I am rushed through emergency and upstairs to labor where I hear through my altered state hushed allusions to an emergency C-section, something we have never even read literature on. My body—on its own or because of my fear—goes into near paralysis. The contractions, that have become lighter and fewer, all but cease.

For as long as I can remember, I have had the vague belief in the back of my mind that I will die at thirty, and now here I am thirty years old and I am sure I will die in surgery. I go into a panic. I plead with the staff to please, please let me have my baby naturally. "I don't want to die," I beg them. "Please don't make me go into surgery to die."

But with no contractions and no progress, surgery is the only option. The surgeon, Dr. Blass, who has been called and is listening to all this, approaches the gurney, lowers his head down to meet my eyes through his black-rimmed glasses and says in a hoarse, irritated voice, "Listen, lady, I haven't lost a patient except to cancer in twenty years and I'm not about to spoil my record with you. You and your baby will die without surgery. Now stop screaming and let's move on."

Robert is holding my hand and looks strong and loving. "You'll be okay," he says. "You and our baby will be okay."

And the next morning, shocked to find myself alive, I am aware of excruciating pain in my stomach and a twilight, unreal sense of the world around me, until the nurse says she will bring in my baby and then . . . . Love at first sight was never like this.

Kira is five and a half pounds little, small bones and thin skin, but oh my god, a true, real, warm child is here in my arms, on my breast, and as my milk tries to flow I am stricken and will never stop loving this being who has conquered my heart with no more than the essence of her being and need, needing me to give her life, attention, the basics of survival and more than anything a holding place for the love she will get and give for the rest of her life. I am in awe of this miracle of skin and bones, the heart thumping away at my heart, the tiny, still wrinkly fingers and toes, the black knot where the umbilical chord has been cut, the once in a while opening blue eyes and the small mouth rubbing back and forth finding the nipple on my breast.

It is for Kira that I write a lullabye, *Child of My Dreams*, bringing a source of creativity I have never tapped into at this level. It becomes a song I sing to Chanti, our youngest daughter, and to close friends and even clients at times when they are in deepest need of reparenting.

Child of my dreams
I love you so,
While you are sleeping
Your dreams can grow.

Stars will be shining
The moon will be rising
The sun will be waiting
To bring a sweet morning.

Child of my dreams
I love you so
While you're asleep
My love will grow.

Whether the moon
Or the stars are in heaven
Dreams of our friendship
Are closer than ever.

Child of my dreams
I love you so,
While you are sleeping
Your dreams can grow.

WE HAVE NO parenting skills, but are determined to be different from our parents. Mother was born in 1913 in Poland, at a time when obeying an authority's instructions without question could mean the difference between life and death. And so, in the 1940's, when the experts warned against coddling a child and had precise time standards for digestion and elimination, Mother followed the rules. While she did nurse for a few months, it was on a tight schedule, as was holding a baby. Once, later in life, recounting her battles with her own mother, she gave me a transparent view of my childhood. "No matter how many times I told her to let you cry it out, your grandmother would pick you up and hold you as soon as I turned my back. I kept explaining that crying it out was the way to get you regular, but she refused to listen to me. It made me furious."

As I listen to my new daughter's heartbeat and the sound of her cries, I cannot understand how my mother could ignore the child in front of her and follow experts from a distance, no matter what her past. I have no specific parenting skills yet, but I am certain that I will continue to respond to Kira's needs as she expresses them.

I think about how Mother earned a Bachelor of Science degree going to City College at night while working full-time. Once, when I was in high school, in a rare moment of vulnerability, she showed me several sensitive and delicate portraits she had drawn in pencil and charcoal and a few sweet, humble stories about her life that she had written when she was my age.

It is hard to reconcile her abrupt and harsh exterior with the young person she was before she opted for accounting over literature in order to support her parents, who were unable to find steady work during the depression. She never wrote stories or did artwork again. Whoever supported Mother and her needs? Perhaps my Father isn't the only tragic figure in my family.

I AM ALMOST finished with my Masters in Social Work. I have just one course, clinical work and a thesis left. Classes have seemed irrelevant to the world, the wards, the clinics, the pain, the people involved. Teachers have been often boring and unable to get along even among themselves. And I, of course, am still often unstable and intolerant, so how can I criticize? Yet I do.

Kira, a few months old, comes to class with me and her small tufts of white hair, curious fists and tiny mouth nursing make the hours in class tolerable. A woman in the class whispers that the only reason she bothers to come is to see my daughter grow. Kira watches everything with her almond blue eyes, making sense and nonsense indistinguishable.

This course is called Abnormal Behavior and we are each to do a presentation on a neurosis, character disorder or psychosis, as if they are universal, clearly defined categories. I volunteer to report on manic depression, which I figure I have something to say about. But it turns out I don't have the stamina or the heart to follow through on self-disclosing. I go to the library and read several psychology journals with dull articles that deal with my Father's diagnosis and I report on symptomology and medication. I say nothing about the inner world of my Father, his struggles and abuse. My report is informative, surface, boring; a travesty and betrayal.

Fieldwork is better. I can experience and learn through watching, trying, failing and sometimes succeeding. Regardless of my impact on them, the clients I see leave their images and struggles indelibly on my heart.

JULIA, HER EYES are like ice in her stiff face. She dares me to make her well. She puts her arm around me in the waiting room and jaunts along the hall this way. She makes certain I know she will set the rules. And I may not trespass her walls. I am unnerved, cannot respond properly, carefully or caringly. I am overwhelmed by her stiff face and her pretense. I want to tell her that I can help her, that I want to spare her from the hospital, more electric shock in her brain. I want to tell her of my Father, that he, too, would not listen, would not risk, would not try. And of what has become of him. What has?

I am her therapist and she looks at me with a tight smile on her face. "Can I help you?" she asks me, blurring our roles. What am I to say? She is sixty years old and perhaps tender and thoughtful in a real sense as my Father was and as Mother could not be. I want to share this with her. My dilemma. That I want her to be my parent. Hush. What would they say, all of them, the competent, traditional, controlled ones. What did it matter?

Julia, perhaps we could have been direct about where we were starting and where we could go from there. I was afraid, afraid of my own needs, of wanting you to change or to remain too much the same.

We sit across and you tell me you are feeling fine and you are not depressed since the shock treatment but that you feel rigid because of the medication. We change the medication and some of the rigidness, the frozen quality, leaves. But where do we go? You have no problems, you insist, and yet your husband says you sit in your rocking chair and stare for many hours. How can I help you if you will not share how you are inside the reserved eyes?

I see you with your husband for several weeks and it is easier. He is in touch with his fears and his needs. I speak mostly with him, knowing it is you I need to talk with. We all silently assent to this farce.

One week I see you alone. You say he could not come. I am afraid to be alone with you for a whole hour, but I do not tell you this. We talk slowly, hesitantly. We talk about your husband some and you say he talks too much. I ask you about this and you say you tell him and that it is all right. The door closes. I ask you what you want to work on and you say things are going well and there is no reason to come in. I feel upset. Frustrated. Don't you know this will happen again? I want to say. Don't you know about my Father and those like him, returning, returning, returning?

I do not say this. I ask Julia a question about her childhood and she says that she does not like to think of her past but does not mind if it will help me. I jump on this. "Help me?" I say with a soft voice and smile but she knows, she knows the fury behind the words. "Well, help you to help me," she says in an equally soft voice, her eyes hardening, hard and wooden in her face. She is finished, she will not return. I grow more furious. Frustrated that I am wrong, doing this all wrong. I confront her. "You know you have some serious problems," I tell her. "You are the one who needs help, that is why you are here." Her eyes are black. "Yes," she says submissively. "I know." But she is closed to me forever. She will never come back again. Afraid to accept her as she was, to accept her help, to earn her trust. To allow her, Julia, to allow my Father, to be.

A T THE CRISIS clinic, a man with a glazed strangeness in his eyes, sitting on a metal folding chair, trying to suppress his energy. His face is locked into an expression of cynicism but he is unable to stop his body movements or his eyes from darting around the room, staring at people around him.

Mark, on duty, says to me, "Have you ever been to the Med Center?" I shake my head and he asks if I'd like to ride out with him in the mobile unit. We get our jackets and Mark tells the man to come on.

"This is an easy case," Mark tells me as we walk down the hall, past Emergency and X-Ray and into the lot.

The man has risen jauntily from his chair and is walking separately from us. I notice the peculiar way he holds his arms, rigidly swinging, stiffened almost in a boomerang as he walks. I notice but do not associate.

I am afraid of this man; he looks as if he is ready to explode. He sits in the back seat and I push the button down on the door, then get in on my side. Mark tells him we will be at the Med Center soon and he says, "It's all right, all right," in a forced casual voice. He does not smile, but is stiff and seems unpredictable.

Mark and I talk of neighborhoods and camping. The man moves around uneasily in the back seat. He is having trouble keeping his cool and is becoming more agitated. I pretend he is not there. And there is no reason to be anxious. He is where he wants to be . . . he is going home.

We walk into the Med Center and over to the admissions desk, the man following behind us. Mark tells the receptionist the man's name and that he has been here before and is going in on a voluntary admission.

"I see," she says, smiling maternally, as the man approaches the desk. She takes out a long triplicate form and places it in her typewriter. She begins to ask him questions.

"Your name, sir?" she asks brightly.

He answers her as if he is applying for a job and is proud of his credentials.

She has set the tone and he continues it, accentuates it, glaring it out for passersby to see. His voice is too loud but he is not aware of this. His energy is erupting. The form is detailed. The dialogue continues in this manner, she never losing her bright, superficial tone, he pushing out his tight words in loud, hostile sounds.

Finally it is over. He compresses somewhat. She gives him a pen and asks him to sign his name. Grandiloquently he writes his signature on the line, committing himself to the hospital's care for seventy-two hours, or more.

The woman calls the ward and asks for the doctor who worked with him last time he was there.

We wait. The woman does her work. The man taps on the counter. Mark speaks of nothing and I pretend to listen, safe now but still with fear.

A polished face and voice appear out of the elevator. The doctor approaches the man and puts his arm around his shoulder. "Hey there, Frank, good to see you," he says cheerfully. Frank laughs aloud, relieved, finally noticed, recognized. "Hey there, Doc," he says and puts out his hand. "Put her there." The doctor shakes hands warmly and asks how he has been and the man says, "Fine, you know, I'm just super these days."

The doctor asks him where his baseball hat is and the man looks at him without understanding. "Don't you remember?" the doctor says, "Last time you were here you were carrying all kinds of equipment and were wearing your baseball uniform."

The doctor is laughing and I begin to feel tense and stiff. It begins to occur to me that he is laughing at this man. He is not being friendly; he is enjoying this man's strangeness.

The man makes an awkward motion with his mouth as if he is trying not to laugh or scream. "That's right," he says, and lifts his hand to his head. He begins to laugh. "You know you're right. I remember now." And his laugh gets louder, though he does not seem to believe it is funny.

I don't think it's funny. I feel angry at the doctor and helpless at the same time. At least he is relating to the man. Not quiet and anxious like I am. I begin to feel even more anxious and suddenly very tired. Things are beginning to add up and my feelings are tearing me apart. The strange look in his eyes, the swing of the arms, the tenseness, the idiosyncratic humor.

We go up in the elevator and he and the doctor talk as Mark and I listen. The words do not matter, they sometimes don't make sense, but it is obvious they are relating at some level.

Upstairs Mark asks if this isn't quite a place and I look around, impressed in spite of myself. Things are clean and neat and there are only two patients to a room. There is strong sunlight and some warm colors from prints and lamps. The doctor brings the man in, tells him where he is to stay. "Welcome home," he says.

I go back downstairs alone and over to the desk to ask when the man was here before and the receptionist tells me about three months ago. I say that seems like a short time to be out and she says, "Oh, no, it seems long. Some are here every other week."

I anxiously wait with Mark for the doctor to debrief us. After a while he returns and begins to discuss his patient. I let the doctor's words filter meaninglessly through my mind, waiting for a pause so I can ask for the man's clinical diagnosis, even though I already know.

GINGER COMES IN, twenty-four years old, hunched over, makeup smeared around her mouth and lids, her dress hanging on her body. She is sobbing, impatient, unwilling to try again.

"Meds," she tells me. "I want meds. I've had my fill of therapy. All I want is meds."

She tells me of her past. She has tried to kill herself several times, once becoming comatose for nine days. She has lost a child, a marriage, a job, and does not care about anything anymore.

"I don't want you to die," I tell her, identified with her pain, pain in this child of twenty-four. I feel the tears in my own eyes as I feel her hopelessness, her self-abuse. She looks at me in almost disbelief. She tests me out, is hard, soft, distant and close. I do not give her medication. I tell her I want to help her handle the hurt, not shut the pain up with a pill. She is angry, abusive. She gathers her dress to her, and crying bitterly, leaves the office and slams the outer door. "I am sorry," I whisper, "so sorry."

But she has not given up. There is a small section of her that will try if she can find some hope. She calls, comes in. She is suspicious and guarded. Her lipstick is on straighter, though, and her posture is not quite as strange. We talk; talk some more. We begin to reach each other.

A few weeks later, a call. "A job! I have a job!" Hope back in her voice, the beginnings, the embryonic structures of life. Someone—I—believed in her. She has begun to trust.

I do not recognize this girl, who comes in differently each week. She has no abnormality in her back once she feels pride in standing straight. Her hair is delicate, her features soft, her eyes warm. Slowly, slowly, she begins to live. "You understand me," she says, "and have reached me like no one else has been able to."

We have worked hard together. I have confronted her on her intolerance, self-abuse, and isolation. I have held her when she mourned for the baby she gave up five years ago. Have suffered with her when she told of her parents' rejection of her, too much for them to bother with: "I learned real young," she says, "to be nice . . . but, god, it is good to be so much more than just nice!"

She is all right now. One of the survivors. She writes me letters sometimes. She tells me she has earned her "people credential" with me, and suspects how hard I have worked to earn mine. Her letters are serious and comic and loving. She is a person evolving. And I have helped her to be this.

At the bottom of one of her letters she writes: P.S. I'm finding out there is room for me. There is enough to go around.

I have always wanted to help my Father in this way; I never knew how. Without his pain I would never have helped this woman. In an indirect way, he has helped her, too.

Would this make any sense, hold any meaning for my Father? I wish he were here and I could share this with him.

Mahler strings music, disconnected and dissonant, together and it all winds into oneness. It all connects for me somehow. I wish my Father and I were in the same dimension of sound and it connected for him, too.

THE MEN AND women in the group I am learning to co-lead as part of my internship at a day treatment center wear labels, mostly "Schizophrenic" or "Paranoid." They hear voices that frighten them, telling them they are being followed or poisoned or need to be punished. They are taking cocktails of psychotropic medications to attempt to control the voices or at least lower their volume. A common theme in sessions is how to get rid of the voices, and people share their methods: arguing with the voices, ignoring the voices, thanking the voices, screaming back at them, banging their heads against a wall. Patricia, a bent over woman in black with thick glasses and too much orange lipstick, says that music turned up high with headphones on works way better than the meds and there is a chorus of "Oh yeah!" and nods of tired agreement around the room.

Most of the group members function for varying periods of time as out-patients in group homes or with family and then go back to the ward for 72 hours or a couple of weeks. I can't tell if they are in remission now because mental illness tends to be cyclical, because therapy and connection help, or if there are some good uses for meds. I wish I knew what kind, how much, or what effects or side effects the drugs are adding to the load these people already carry from their histories, current lives and mental states.

I ask Jeff, my mentor therapist, for more information about the drugs, trying to covertly gather information about my Father, should he ever show up. Jeff knows little, he admits, and says he wishes he knew more, but the social work staff is supposed to leave medications up to the psychiatrist who, he informs me bitterly, sees his patients for under fifteen minutes, once a month—if they're lucky.

And then the picture of my Father comes into focus. My Father being fed psychotropic medications—sometimes intramuscularly—sometimes when he is too depressed to argue—and sometimes when he is stopped from cheeking or trading meds for small objects or extra desserts to other patients on the ward. The blanket control of psychiatrists, most of whom have neither time, inclination nor energy to offer a shred of humanity to people in pain, the ignorance of my peers, and my own ignorance combine to rise up and make me sick.

So when it's time to start on my masters project, I decide to find out if other social workers, family therapists, and psychologists know as little as I do about drugs, uses, indications, dosages and side effects; and whether or not they care. When I talk to Judine, a friend in class, about my project she offers to co-write it and we get approval from the department to go ahead. We construct a simple three-page survey that we send out to a hundred and fifty clinicians in California, chosen randomly from the phone book.

We get an unheard of high return rate and the data from the survey are astounding. Over 95% of those surveyed admit to knowing little or nothing about the psychotropic drugs their clients are ingesting and about the same number say yes they would definitely appreciate more information and yes, a handbook for clinicians would be welcome. Yes, they would be happy to pay for it. When and where can they buy it?

We consign ourselves to learning about psychotropic medications from the thick, abstruse, cumbersome *Physicians Desk Reference* and it is here that I find the description of the spasdic locking jaw movements that have intermittently plagued my Father when he tried to swallow food; uncontrollable movements that became more severe over time with the accumulation of the medications' toxic effects in his system. The convulsive jaw motion had a name and a cause: Tardive Dyskenesia, a common side effect from the shock treatments and toxic major tranquilizers, mostly given intramuscularly, to shut him up.

A perfect, horrific example of iatrogenic—physician treatment induced—disease.

The intermittent spasms or seizures during meals increased in intensity as time went by. The interesting thing was that when he was high they completely disappeared.

Not that it matters now. For all I know, my Father is in the morgue or underground.

Busy being moms, Judine and I complete our masters project and graduate, but we never follow through on creating a drug manual. It is many years before handbooks for the lay public come out. And I don't understand nearly enough to be of help to those clients on medication who are entrusting me with their lives.

DEAR LORD! MOTHER has known for months that my Father is alive but didn't tell me because she didn't want me to get upset.

PART THREE

FOUND

The Three Stories House

MOTHER'S CONSCIENCE HAS gotten the better of her and she calls to tell me that my Father is alive and not even hospitalized. He has, in fact, been visiting Aunt Ruth every couple of weeks.

"How long have you known?"

"A few months. I wanted to spare you. I'm sorry."

I am furious at Mother for keeping this from me and telling Aunt Ruth not to call me. I have spent most of the last five years assuming my Father was dead.

Yet several more months pass and even though I can now contact my Father, I do not. I find reasons not to call. He is doing all right now. He is stable. I don't want to disrupt anything.

The real reason though is I am afraid to talk to him after so many years. For all of my protestations of love and concern, for all of my bravado, I am afraid to again have to face the depression unto death, the mad laughter, the silver-blue eyes with their piercing need and erratic moods. And I don't want all my knotted-up feelings for my Father unbound and opened and twisted up again.

I am afraid that if I call Aunt Ruth he will be there and I will have to talk to him. I have never known what to say when he was depressed. How will I know now? If he is high he will bring all his problems into my newly secure existence, safe from chaos and incoherence.

What good will it do my Father if I call, anyway? The past is done. What can I offer him besides lost, unhappy memories?

AND NOW THERE is no need to make the call. It comes to me. Aunt Ruth is on the line. "I've picked up the phone to call so many times."

I don't even ask how she is. All I can focus on is my Father, certain something horrible has happened. "Aunt Ruth, how is my Father?"

"Well, not so good," she answers. "He's in the hospital again. Not Brooklyn State this time—the one on Wards Island—Manhattan State I think it's called. He was making trouble for people—just nuisance stuff you know, but he got arrested and when he got to jail he told them he'd come from the nuthouse. So first they brought him to Kings County and now he's out there on Wards Island. They won't take him at Brooklyn State because his address is in Manhattan."

He must have been high. That's better than being depressed, as far as I am concerned. But Manhattan State—the isolation of Wards Island! We'd always given Aunt Ruth's address in Brooklyn so he could go to Brooklyn State, where things were familiar to him and where it was close enough for us to visit.

"How long has he been in Manhattan State?"

"Maybe a few weeks."

"You've seen him?"

"I can't travel that far, not with my health. I talk to him on the phone. He's doing all right. Just lonely."

I should have called sooner. I should have known this would happen. Now here he is in some god-forsaken place on some island an hour and a half from Brooklyn and no one there. I might have helped my Father, but despite all my grandiose plans and protestations, when it comes down to reality, I do not even bother to call.

AFTER SEVERAL ATTEMPTS, I get through, not to my Father but to my Father's psychiatrist at Manhattan State Hospital. They have written down that he has organic brain syndrome, because when he was high he lied and said he had convulsions. They have down that he has a heart condition and diabetes because when he was high he checked things randomly on the list.

His main diagnosis though is psychiatric: schizophrenia, chronic, undifferentiated. I can feel the familiar rage at the incompetence of psychiatrists, putting bizarre, unsubstantiated information together to create a muddled, lunatic chart that has nothing to do with my Father. I find out that they have him on a low dose of Thorazine, which is mostly making him tired. Better than Elavil—all we need is another distended bladder. And fortunately, they are overcrowded and he has not been disruptive enough for them to force electric shock treatments on him.

I carefully tell the doctor that the chart (not he) is incorrect; that my Father is not schizophrenic. I state this in a calm and professional voice, so he will not shut me out. "My Father was diagnosed manic-depressive when he was thirty-three," I tell him. "Twenty-nine years ago. He has had episodes of mania and depression every few years since." The doctor is not sure what to believe. I add details. I tell him of the time my Father was put on exhibit for a group of psychology students so they could see a real live manic-depressive in action.

I use my credentials. I am a social worker with experience working in hospitals. I share my personal experience: I have lived with my Father's manic depression since I was five. I tell him that if he can get my Father's chart from Brooklyn State Hospital, the diagnosis will be verified, in black and white.

The psychiatrist tells me then that he had considered the possibility that my Father was manic-depressive but ruled it out because my Father denied ever getting depressed. I tell him what is dawning on him: that my Father is not about to admit he has depressed feelings when he is high.

At least this doctor seems only unaware and overworked, not brutal, and he is trying to listen. I try to straighten out the rest of the mess. I request that my Father's chart be reviewed, because I've never known him to have convulsions, diabetes, or heart problems. The conversation has shifted; it feels more like a consultation that I might be doing at the crisis clinic at UC Davis Medical Center where I have interned. We begin to talk about blood tests to establish tolerance levels to try lithium. And finally this call is over, draining me of even my bitterness and anger.

I call Aunt Ruth and update her on my Father. I offer to pay for a cab so she can go and see him but when I hear her hesitation I tell her not to worry about it. She is seventy-five years old and it's a long distance to go by yourself. Who am I to ask her to visit? He is my Father, I am healthy and I have not gone to see him. I still haven't even called him. In actual fact, I keep my world, three thousand miles away, peaceful and I continue to shut my Father out.

THESE DAYS ARE heaven for me. I love my home and my family. A wild artichoke has gone to flower, thin silken threads of lavender rest on a quilt of green leaves over a thick stalk. Tomatoes, zucchini, cucumbers, peppers and eggplant ripen in the garden boxes we built. Humingbirds add color, sound and movement to the easy afternoon. Robert is upstairs writing and two-year-old Kira is asleep in her wooden crib.

This morning a neighbor came by to see if we wanted to walk to the park nearby and I was grateful that she knew that our home was open, that she could drop in without notice or invitation.

No one stopped by our apartment. Occasionally we would have company, one of Mother's friends from high school or college. Except for his childhood friend, Danny, who never came to visit because Mother did not like him, my Father didn't seem to have friends. We saw my Father's family at their homes, not ours. I rarely brought my few friends home.

Mother would spend hours cleaning our apartment before anyone visited, even though we had only three rooms and few furnishings and it wasn't ordinarily dirty or in disarray. I can see Mother on her knees to get the floors spotless, her hair disheveled, her mouth tight, wearing my Father's navy and brown bathrobe over her full slip. I can see her, clearly, scrubbing away, resenting us sitting there without helping, my Father reading the paper and me drawing and listening to music.

When my Father did pitch in and clean the bathroom or the kitchen, Mother would watch him surreptitiously and redo the parts he did wrong. When he was gone, she would tell me in an annoyed, impatient tone that she would just as soon he didn't help at all, since he did such a careless job. At first I defended him, but she would purse her lips tighter and not listen. Eventually I stopped arguing, just salvaged my pride by refusing to help her, knowing she judged me as she did my Father.

WHILE I WAIT to hear reports of my Father's state of being, new life is forming within me. Kira is by now an easygoing almost three-year-old and I am lucky and grateful to continue to be a stay-at-home mom with my only commitments to a play group and working one morning every other week as a parent helper at the pre-school nearby. In so many ways we are living the best of my dreams. Robert's job is stable and we have enough money to pay our low mortgage and enjoy our simple lifestyle. We can't wait to meet our second child.

We are in our long grass-filled backyard, with orange trees, grapefruit, loquats, small shrubs and an oak tree, wild onions, roses, camellias, azaleas and pink ladies that crop up once in a while. The vegetable boxes are waiting to be filled again with tomatoes, egg-plant, peppers, melons, cukes, squash and strawberries.

Robert is reaching up to pick oranges from our tree on this unusually warm sunny afternoon in early March, less than a month before our child is due. Kira helps Robert collect oranges in a paper bag so we can make juice with our hand juicer, and I lie resting on our rope and fabric hammock in the afternoon sun.

Kira and I are wearing matching outfits that I have sewed for us: a green plaid long skirt with an expandable waist insert and a vest for me to wear over a blouse; a skirt and a vest for her.

The insert of my skirt is stretched almost as far as it can go. Robert walks over to one of our camellias with his clippers and snips a huge, perfect red flower with its leaves framing it and he and Kira walk over to me to show and tell. I don't remember whose idea it was to lower the elastic down from my stomach and balance the flower in the center, but Robert goes in the house and gets his 35 mm camera and snaps this moment out of time, all of us rapt in the symbolism, beauty and anticipation of the new life waiting to be born.

We are prepared to be a family of four. We have learned parenting skills that we believe make us better parents. Robert and I are trying to keep perspective on the ways our patterns sometimes make us clash and irritate each other.

I have shown Kira the pictures in *A Child Is Born*, the book I read when I was pregnant with her: the small walnut-size amorphous being; the six-month-old fetus with its thumb in its mouth, like hers is when she waits and watches or goes to sleep at night. Kira has been practicing being a good big sister with her dolly.

It's hard to think about my Father on days like these.

DRUNKS AND DERELICTS SITTING under trees, talking and gesturing in the heat. I want to take a shortcut with my children through the park but I am afraid to. The thought flashes through my mind uninvited: Why don't they clean up the parks so that decent people can use them? We, the civilized, want everything. All of the parks.

I was one of the vagrants when I was with my Father, lying down under the trees and scaring off the socialized ones, indiscernible from those who have nothing and have little to offer or hope for. Why should I be afraid of these people, of myself and my Father? But I have worked hard for what I have. I do not want it taken away from me.

I try to imagine what my Father has been doing these past, lost years, before he returned to the hospital. Aunt Ruth told me he had been working as a messenger on Wall Street and I had let it sink into unconsciousness. Now it comes to me as an intrusion, as moving images. I picture my Father taking letters and packages from a pompous business-suited young man, after waiting for him in the paneled, polished room. He is marginally high and interested, fascinated with the businesses and charts and action, as if he is sightseeing. He delivers the items, collects a tip, goes on to another place and repeats the process. Runners, they call the messengers. Runners for the civilized people who have made it. But perhaps my Father does not mind—even brags to himself or others at the agencies about the places he has seen, as if he were a significant part of the setting.

I recall runners coming to the office during the short time I worked in publishing. Some looked content with what they were doing, but others looked despairing or hostile. I can also imagine my Father going from place to place depressed and lethargic, not looking at people, handing packages to unknown hands silently, his coat collar pulled up around his neck, his mouth pressed tight, eyes ringed black.

Which image fits my Father? Was he either or both or entirely different? He is not an image anyway. He is a person with his own internal world, and I may not know its contents.

I PAINT MY Father in my fantasy home that I have called *The Three Stories House*. It is a cross section of our home, and you can view inside the rooms like an open dollhouse. The house has greenery around it and the sky is a smoky gray and blue, the sun and moon present at the same time.

My Father is a gray and white translucent spirit in clouds in an irregularly shaped room on the left side of the chimney on the third story that floats over the roof. I paint Mother sitting in a straight chair in the clouds on the other side of the chimney. On the second story, Kira, three years old, and Chanti, a few months, are playing in Kira's room with Snoodles, our border collie, and on the first floor Robert and I are embracing. I tell these three stories, imagining I have been able to create a safe place for my Father and Mother.

Perhaps my Father does not mind his life as it is that much. Danny finally visited and said he is not as bad as he could be. What does that mean? He is no longer high, and now he rarely speaks and never asks for anything. He waits for the days to pass, with little expected, nothing hoped for.

I spend hours fantasizing about my Father's world, but what does he care for my fantasies?

Surely I do not enter his.

My Father's influence on me is never-ending. I am linked to him daily, as I try to grow strong and close to Robert, yet become mired in old feelings. We speak of our increasing distance, our anger. "Why are we fighting, Robert?" I ask, discouraged, hardly caring. And slowly I remember my Father lying on our couch, depressed for weeks and months, self-absorbed, self-involved, not able to care for me at all. Well, how could he? I defend him to no one but myself. He was in despair. I know.

My extreme need to be loved is dumped on Robert, this insatiable, long-ago denied need. So we fight. He is tired, and I do not hear his tiredness, only that he does not care, as my Father did not care. I approach wanting to make love, my hair combed smooth, my eyes direct, and Robert does not see and understand—and we fight. I do not tell him of my need, only of his insensitivity, and we go on and on. How continually we conjure up this fight. But not always. Sometimes I allow myself to receive love and sometimes Robert is able to offer it.

How irrelevant this analysis would be to my Father, who never spoke about relationships, even when he was my steady, protective Father. Words, has no one anything to offer but words? I am sorry, Father. Truly I wish I had more for you than paintings and words.

ACTUAL CONVERSATIONS WITH my Father, on the phone finally instead of in my head, vary from slightly uncomfortable to filled with silences. Between him and his assigned social worker, Mrs. Ryder, I find out that he is stable, state hospital program offerings are all alike but he rarely attends and he is definitely down from his manic state. He is waiting to be transferred out of Manhattan State, a process that has taken several long weeks. "Just paperwork," Mrs. Ryder explains to me, an explanation that makes no sense.

Last time I talked to my Father, I didn't realize Kira was in the room. "Who are you talking to?" she asked and when I hung up I showed her the picture of my Father that I keep in my wallet, a close-up I took years ago in New York. "That's your other granddaddy," I told her, "that you've never seen. Perhaps you will meet him one day." My Father is deep in the shadows; his wide eyes are dark and unhappy. But Kira loved him on sight. She was so excited, she didn't want to put the picture down. She carried it around with her carefully and asked again and again, "That's my other granddaddy? And I will see him sometime? I will?" I felt so good about that, I hardly know why. Perhaps because I have good memories of my Father's affection for me as a small child. Loving memories, too, of my own grandfather generously letting me braid his short, sparse gray hair when my grandmother would not let me touch the long white hair that she kept braided in a bun.

I wish I could ask my Father about his parents, the grandparents I never knew. I wish we could spend hours together and he would recount stories of his childhood and his past.

I would like Kira and Chanti, born safely and without surgery a few months ago, to meet my Father, their other granddaddy, and see for themselves not the blackness but the silver-blue color, and the gentleness, so like theirs, in his eyes.

LAST WEEK, MRS. Ryder tells me, my Father, in an open ward, left the hospital with another patient who had a few dollars in his pocket. They called a cab, went to a bar in town, got cokes and listened to music. When the place closed down at 1:00 a.m. they had a problem: They didn't have any money left for a cab. "So they stood outside and waited for a patrol car to cruise by, told the police who they were and the police obligingly took them back to Manhattan State," she says. "They seem fine after their adventure." Unfortunately, though, they lost the privilege of being on an open ward, and no longer have the freedom to come and go as they like. A move out of Manhattan State, soon, seems more important than ever.

Once, when I signed my Father out of Brooklyn State Hospital for the afternoon, we went to a neighborhood nearby with local stores and restaurants and decided to get something to eat. The only trouble was I had only two dollars and some change, and my Father had nothing. That didn't deter my Father. He swooped us into a fancy delicatessen and ordered us a large bowl of vegetable soup for thirty-five cents with two bowls and "a lot of bread." The waiter didn't blink, got our order and brought about six huge pieces of Jewish rye bread with the soup and two bowls so we could share. My Father grinned at him and he smiled back. We listened to the background music and shared the soup and we each had a slice of bread, then wrapped the four extra slices in a napkin, paid, leaving a small tip, and left the restaurant. My Father then steered me into a grocery store, took a package of cream cheese from the shelf and weighed out a quarter pound of grapes "for jelly," he said and despite our small amount of cash we sat on a bench and enjoyed delicious cream cheese and grape jelly sandwiches, which we ate cheerfully under a wide tree.

Are these connected? Only in the way my Father could forget formality and conventionality and be spontaneously playful. Mother would have panicked if she didn't have enough change to get home, but he just waited for a patrol car to pick him up. Mother would have said, "we'd better skip lunch," if there wasn't enough money to eat a regular meal, but my Father created a gourmet lunch.

I wonder where I am in all this. Sometimes I feel I would give up everything for safety and security; other times I would give up everything for a few moments of craziness. I walk the thin edge, and sample some of each, careful not to get too close to the treacherous outer borders.

LAST NIGHT ROBERT and I talked for a while before bed. Things seemed to be all right and I felt good after painting class. But then Robert out of the blue said he thought there was some kind of curse on us because we have a minor rash on our faces. He was just being dramatic, but it made me uneasy and anxious and soon I became conscious of a high, thin, whistling noise in the air. I tried to make it go away by shaking my head, banging my head with my palm. "I am afraid," I tell Robert. "I can't seem to stop this noise in my head." Outside the wind sounded like choral voices. My hands began to go limp and I started sweating. I began to panic. The familiar fear of being, going, out of my mind, of being my Father.

Get away, Father, I write in my journal. Get away.

The whistling will not go away. I go into another room, turn on the light. It is better with the light on. A distraction from sound. I read the editorials, the daily complaints and suggestions. The sound lessens. I pick up my journal again and attempt to harness my fear. Finally, tired, I go back to bed to be with Robert.

"I am going downstairs for a minute to close up," he says.

"No. Stay with me. Hold me."

He turns and holds me and we both fall asleep.

This morning it seems silly, less threatening. I am in the kitchen making breakfast, almost cheerful. The noise begins again, but this time I follow the sound, trace it to the real world. It is coming from the refrigerator, between cycles. I am only picking up the high sounds with increased hypersensitivity. The washing machine has the same sound. It is real, not in my head. What is in my head is the exaggeration of the sound, the focus, and the preoccupation with insanity. Probably I am borderline something-or-other (I am terrified by the words) but it does not matter. My senses are more acute than most other people's, that is all, that is ALL that it means.

Go with it. Do not panic. Remember that this world is not a known place, not solidly known by anyone, not the sane or the insane. The levels of the world are incomprehensible: reality cut off through the capriciousness of chance, time, temperatures, senses, and scores of unknowns.

M Y FATHER'S TRANSFER finally comes through, and his new home, in Brooklyn, is called River Court Convalescent Hospital. It's close enough for Aunt Ruth and Danny to visit.

I talk to Mrs. Hirsch, my Father's current social worker, and she tries to give me an update on my Father. "Let's see...." she says. "He doesn't speak much to anyone. I don't think he's bedridden, but he isn't participating in activities. I can find out more details from the staff and call you back next week—it's hard to keep track of all the patients here." She tells me there are only two social workers for 180 residents. I listen to her as she brushes off layers of guilt as if it were dust, so she has room to accumulate more tragedy, more complaints, more inhumanity to man. We set a date to talk in a week. She will get more information for me from the nurses who know my Father as someone to give custodial care to, from the psychiatrist's notes and perhaps even from my Father, if she can make time to visit the third floor.

Aunt Ruth calls me after visiting my Father at River Court. She begins with her usual description of her pains and the arthritis in her toes that will have to be treated soon. I interrupt her after a while and ask, "How is he?"

Aunt Ruth pauses, hesitates. "Well . . . he's quiet . . . you know how he gets when he's quiet. I guess the best way I can describe it is that . . . he's forlorn. You know what I mean? Remember when he was in that Catholic hospital and he wasn't eating or anything? Well, he's not that bad, he eats by himself now, thank God, and he speaks a little, but you know—he seems forlorn. I don't know how else to describe it."

What a haunting word for depressed: forlorn. I don't know what to say.

"He looks a lot older," she continues. "He's thinner than he used to be. And he's more gray and bald.

"But he had a good appetite. I went to the delicatessen by my house and I told the man that I needed the sandwich to take to the hospital for my brother and I didn't know till we got there, but he gave me a sandwich that was like a double sandwich, there was so much meat, and your father, God bless him, ate almost the whole thing, just left a little corner at the end. Next time I go to see him I'm going to bring him a pastrami sandwich. That's what he wants next time, a pastrami sandwich."

"Did he tell you that?" I ask. Every piece of minutiae significant in the paucity of words, in the parched center of my throat. What is it like inside my Father's soul? Is pastrami more significant than corned beef?

"Well, I asked him if he wanted it and he nodded. And Danny—you know Danny was there too—Danny told him he would bring him hot dogs from Nathan's next time he came, and he smiled at that. The way he used to smile, you know. Danny is gray, too. Still good-looking and dressed real fine, but his hair is also gray. We're all getting older. I'm seventy-five, no spring chicken." I try to picture my Father as she has described him. Forlorn. Less hair, thin, depressed. Forlorn.

"What is it like there?"

"It's spotless, I wish my kitchen looked like that, it's so clean. I guess it's easy to keep clean because most of the people are in wheel-chairs or in their rooms. We looked for a doctor to talk to, but there was no one there. I guess because it was a weekend and they're all home."

"Does my Father stay in his room all the time, too?"

"He was in the lounge when we got there. I guess he sits by the TV most of the day. Maybe he walks around a little. But he doesn't talk much. Even when we asked him questions he answered a little, but not much."

"His answers make sense?"

"Yeah, but he doesn't talk too much."

"Are there magazines for the patients?"

"No, I didn't see any."

I tell her about the subscription to *Time* I sent and wonder if I should send him another subscription. She tells me that the place is so large she doubts he will ever get it.

"I'll bring him a sports book when I visit again, in a couple of weeks when Max can take me. You remember him? He's the lawyer who helped your Father out a couple of times. He always liked your Father. Well, he said he would bring me to visit Sam in a couple of weeks and I'll bring a sports book then."

I offer again to pay for a taxi so she can visit more often.

"I don't want your money," she says gently. "You keep it, you have children, use it for them."

For some reason, after I hang up the phone, I begin to cry. What is it with this family of mine, these ghosts that hang in gray sheets behind and in front of my life? Goodness and generosity are part of who they are, a gentle kindness that most people I encounter do not possess. Mother rarely understood or treasured this. "Your Father would give anyone the shirt off his back," Mother would say, scornfully. And yet in retrospect I can see that she had a point. After all, she was the one who worked and paid for the shirt.

CHANTI, A YEAR and a half, plays with her food. Her entire diet for the last couple of months has consisted of eggs, cottage cheese, cereal, bananas, rice and cheese, peanut butter, milk and apple juice. Not a bad selection of food, but so limited as to make me concerned about vitamin and mineral deficiencies. Well, she also eats bread and occasionally a bit of broccoli and a carrot. Maybe it's not as bad as it seems at first glance. Anyway, I would like her to try at least some of the foods I prepare. They aren't that awful.

I was so traumatized by being coerced into eating that I can't do that to my children. Unless it's a true safety issue, I believe that I have no right to impose my will on their bodies. How do I know what they need and what they do not? I am not them.

Yet the problem remained until I remembered how my Father used to handle it with me when I would not eat.

"Chanti," I say, "I bet I can drink this shake up faster than you can. Want to race me?" The shake is made with strawberries, cashews, yogurt, bananas, and milk, and I *know* she would like it if she would just taste it.

"Okay," says Chanti, as if it were the most natural thing in the world.

I pour about two ounces of shake into a little glass for her and then some for me. We hold our glasses up.

"On your mark, get ready, get set . . . GO!"

In no time we are both finished, and she is beaming. "Me won, me won, Mommy, and you won, too!"

"Would you like to race again?" I ask and we do, this time with straws, and she giggles as she makes strawberry bubbles around the top of her Big Bird cup.

And, when we are through with that and I ask her if she would like some more shake just to drink, she finishes off the last foamy bit at the bottom of the blender of her own volition.

So simple, my Father's style and way. A concoction she had refused for weeks, and here she was enjoying it and getting good nutrition, too.

We have since raced our way through tastes of lasagna, pizza, cottage cheese and spinach squares, and several other dishes that I was sure she would like if she would try them. To give her credit for having her own mind, she would not (but after tasting it) race through asparagus ("I don't like it.") or tortilla and beans and cheese ("No."). Which is as I would have it. No forcing, no rewards at the end, no punishments, no hostility. My Father's gentle game with everyone the winner.

A PSYCHIATRIC INTERN reads from the psychiatric notes:
    Began to refuse medication.

    Lithium reduced to 300 mgs. t.i.d. from 600 mgs. t.i.d.

    Navane 1 mg.

    Prescription is in fact academic.

    Patient is markedly impoverished and seemingly depressed.

    Possibility of intramuscular medication.

Impoverished. Almost, perhaps even more evocative a portrait than forlorn.

I call Mrs. Hirsch to get more details, images.

"Is he still watching TV?" I ask. She says she hasn't seen him in the TV room in a while. "Lately he paces. He walks around the dining room when he's finished eating, walks out on the patio and paces. He paces by the elevator. He doesn't talk but he paces up and down the halls."

There was a wolf I saw once as a child whose fur was torn and gray, whose bones showed underneath. He panted and his eyes were glazed over. Beaten-down is the word: impoverished, forlorn

      pacing around and around in his
      underworld cage.

I could never enjoy the animals again. They were kin.

"My aunt said he's gotten thin. I can't imagine how he looks."

"Well, would it be helpful if I sent you a picture of your Father?"

"A picture . . . ?"

"Yes. There are volunteer aides here and they are glad to take the patients' pictures. It wouldn't be any trouble to send one to you."

Appreciate that. Really would appreciate a picture of my Father. "Please," I reply. "But don't show it to him if it is bad," I tell her.

"Well, maybe I shouldn't send it to you either if you feel it might be too much of a shock."

"No. I want to see it. It will be all right. Send it to me when you get it, please. It is important to me to have it."

She promises she will ask for it that day and send it when the proofs come back. I am shaken up even to consider a tangible picture of my Father. A solid photograph to evaporate or validate the fantasies in my mind.

M Y FATHER'S PICTURE is here. In a stark black and white eight by ten enlargement. A close up of his face down to his chest. A mug shot, out of police files. A convict.

I stare at it, shuddering. This is the best one they could get, they said. Several were discarded first. What is it, besides the obviously uncared-for aura, the disheveled shirt and hair that is so eerie?

I look in his eyes. Something is wrong. His mouth seems to be trying to smile, but his eyes have never considered smiling.

Something else. I cover one side of his face. Not too bad. The right eye looks almost intact. Not enthusiastic or even very alive, but intact. This half of my Father's mouth looks firm but unhappy. Not depressed even, more as if it has seen more than it ever wanted to see, knew more than it ever wanted to know. This side of his face looks congruent.

The other side of his face, the left one, is the incongruent one. His mouth is trying to smile, almost making it, within the dark lined shadows. But the left eye, there is the problem. So many lines on this side of his forehead, eyebrow too deepened at the center, darkness under the eye, shadowing fear and terror, the eye itself expressing pain and resignation, hopelessness and grief. No smile from this eye. No match for the artificially smiling mouth.

All of the parts put together, what a picture. I stare at it for as long as I want to stare. For as long as I can stand.

A LETTER FROM the administration at River Court states that the reimbursement system through the Commissioner of Health has been drastically cut and they will not be able to keep people they cannot make a profit on. "Unless drastic changes are made in the immediate future, the effect of the new program for reimbursement jeopardizes your patient's stay in this facility. In addition it seems likely that the over-all result will be that each family, or concerned person, will have to assume the care and maintenance of their individual relative currently residing at our facility."

It will not happen. They will get an increase in funds.

That place is the end of the line, anyway. My Father would be better off out of there. I will bring him to California. What can we do for him here? He wouldn't even come. Would he?

Who will take care of him if we don't? Aunt Ruth can't. My Father will be released into his own cognizance, and he will leave, off into the shadows, the gray world he knows, that I have not seen. He will be another vagrant, messenger, counterman, non-person, lost in the New York backstreets. And I will never see him again. He will leave and be gone for another seven years or more.

> I should have visited him last summer
> when we knew he was subdued, quiet
> but trapped, caged where we could view him
> like an animal almost
> extinct.
> I want to see my Father.
> I am afraid to see my Father.
> I want to give him a gray room upstairs
> in our imaginary third floor,

> with a bed and a lamp and clothing
> which I will wash every three days
> and he will be safe.

We argue, Robert and I. What would my Father do with all that bickering? He would not like it here.

Mother has moved here, a few miles away. She is not too close, but she is accessible. I can find her if I need to.

Father, be accessible to me.

Do not wander for numberless years.

Do not vanish.

Is it fantasy? I cannot tell. Life has always been too strange for me. Some people seem to understand it so well.

I am afraid for my Father. But I think he would be better off out of that place. It is a place where one waits for death, and you can wait anyplace for that.

Perhaps it will not happen. Perhaps they will find money, and we can put off decisions about where he would be best off. What is another few months of his being depressed and withdrawn. Or forlorn. Or impoverished. Or trapped.

As long as I can see him once before he leaves.

> How dare I
> How dare I wish him caged these months
> for me?

But I do.

Though perhaps it would be easier for all of us if he were gone.

TWO MONTHS HAVE gone by with no further threats of eviction and amazingly in the interim Robert stopped off to see my Father in Brooklyn on his way to Florida to visit his father. He has been there and back, and taken copious notes of the visit for me.

I did not go with him because I am afraid to fly. I believe I will die in a plane crash and I assume that if I keep away (from the spindle, Pandora's box, apples) I will stay alive.

When we first met, I told Robert that my Father used to be a welder and a salesman and left his current employment vague. After a short time, I said we had lost contact and then one time that he had been depressed on and off and eventually I told him the whole story. I was relieved that it didn't make a difference in our relationship or our plans.

"I'm glad I met your Father," Robert tells me. "I understand you more than I could have without this meeting."

Robert's Notes To Me:

Danny picked me up at 10:30. Here's more or less what he said: "I don't know how much you know about Sam's early life. I've known him since we were eleven. We lived next door in Brooklyn. Sold Fuller Brush together. I would say he did moderately well and kept at it. Wearever Aluminum not as good, but kept at it. Then short order cook but didn't care for that. The biggest problem from my view was Lillian pushing him. She was after him to work and impressed me as very dominating. Don't know how she is now but then was control-oriented. Sam was having a hard time and she was not sympathetic. When I visited him in Baltimore she was unfriendly to me. Worse in New York and I didn't understand why. Seemed not to want any men around. A lot of comments about how hard it was to be a mother."

The place was easy to find by car. Pleasant exterior, open atmosphere.

We found Sam upstairs in his room, sleeping. Danny aroused him with some help from attendants who seemed friendly. No feeling of mental institution or wards. Roommate about six feet away. Curtain, semi-private bath, clean, dresser with three drawers, clothes closet with the shirts you sent unused at the bottom, TV at end, windows. Not depressing except nothing to look at outside.

Sam woke up, saw us. Danny introduced us and then I left so he could have time to get oriented to visitors. Danny brought him to the day room in a few minutes. Danny small-talking, sitting between us.

Danny suggested Nathan's. Sam nodded okay. Attendants seemed interested in him having visitors. We observed his pants were stained. "We'll go out and buy you some pants," Danny said. Sam nodded.

Woman attendant said she had seen pictures of Kira and Chanti and that they were real cute. I told her and Sam that I had others and I brought a couple out and showed them around.

Easy to sign out. Also, signed a form authorizing Danny to draw out money to buy what he thought Sam needed.

Nathan's first. Asked what Sam wanted—had to suggest menu. Hot dog, Coke. Then seconds. Seemed hungry. Difficulty eating with mouth problems from the medications. Seemed to enjoy being there but didn't talk.

Drove to Kings Plaza, Macy's. Mentioned birthdays. I halted on your birthdate and he surprised me by supplying the year, then the month and day quickly. Only time he talked for the three hours. Danny asked friendly questions. When he liked something he nodded or said yeah, if not, he said no or shook his head. Most yeses were barely audible. Thought I heard him hum to himself but not sure.

At Macy's, trying on pants took long but he shook his head when asked if he was tired. Hesitated to try pants on, started to put them over shoes. Danny intervened and he caught on, finally tried on three pairs. Fit okay with alterations which were free on pants over $16 which these were. Danny joked about rip-off prices but Sam didn't respond.

Impression though was that he was enjoying outing with his friend and me.

Looked briefly at a sport jacket on his own. Danny asked, "Do you want that, Sam?" Sam shook his head no. Decided to get this another time if he wants it.

Also will get belt, socks, etc., when the altered pants are picked up later in the week. "We'll go back Thursday or Friday, Sam, and get the pants and other things," Danny said. Sam nodded. Danny seemed turned on to more visits, outings and getting Sam some good clothes.

Through all this Sam was not super passive, but somewhat inattentive and just beat-down looking. Shoulders are not stooped but they appear to be when he walks with hands held behind his back. He was not overweight or paunchy. Pants he was in were old and looked bad. New ones looked nice.

Decided to have coffee at Shatkin's Deli near Macy's. Sam nodded for coffee and cheese Danish. He ate it quickly and seemed to enjoy it. Didn't touch coffee. We had egg creams and spoke about original egg creams. Sam was passive. Just out of it for too long—so hard to get back in. Thought he would have liked to look better and was embarrassed. Smiled when I talked to him but it was discouraging that he wasn't talking.

He sat in front of the car going back, seemed to enjoy ride. "Who do you like," Danny had asked earlier, in the day room, "Yankees or Mets?" "Yankees," Sam had answered. But now Danny asked what TV programs he watched and other questions and there was no response.

We went back up to his room. He lay down, looking tired and more flakey.

"I'd like to show you more pictures," I told Sam. Took them out, passed them. He looked, handed them back. Smiled.

Danny left the room letting me say goodbye alone. Said I was sorry the kids and you couldn't be there, but maybe next year. Said I enjoyed taking him out. Then he softly said, "Thank you."

Felt I better leave and not talk more. I asked his roommate in the TV room if Sam ever talked. He said sometimes. Danny was reassured by this but I thought his roommate looked spaced out and unreliable.

Sam impressed me as a gentle, good man, beaten down by continual institutional living and no caring person. Attendant who helped him dress laughed a little when I asked if he needed a lot of coaxing as if yes, he does. They seem supportive in superficial ways, better anyway than most other convalescent hospitals I've seen. But basic impression was still that Sam was lost there.

WITH HIS PLACEMENT at River Court likely to end soon, I have been fixating on what to do with my Father. And now the obsessive ruminating has paid off with a concrete strategy. Why can't we bring him to California and see how it goes? A test drive. Make it clear that it is for only a visit, but have him come out here for a week, ten days, so at least I can see him again. And he can see me and the children. Why not?

"I can't imagine it," Robert says. "He's in a dream. How could he find his way in an airport, on an airplane?"

"That's a terrific idea," Mrs. Hirsch says. "There is a meet-and-assist service at the airlines. They will accompany him getting on and off the planes. People who couldn't travel before have been able to with this service. You wouldn't believe the condition of some of them."

Danny is all for it. He offers to take my Father to the airport, buy clothes, pack for him. "It's certainly worth a try," he says. "There's no hope here."

The social worker, psychiatrist, and Danny each ask my Father if he wants to visit his daughter in California. And clearly, to their amazement, he answers in four words: "Yes, I want to."

And in the real world, in a short while, my Father will be here, and I will view him as if he were a being that I had thought was extinct. I anticipate his visit with a heightened combination of exhilaration and fear.

PART FOUR

HERE

Which One Is The Horse?

I T IS MID-AFTERNOON and we are at Marine World waiting for the plane carrying my Father to arrive at the San Francisco airport a few miles away so he can spend a week and a half with us. It has taken me hours to decide on what to wear. Five-year-old Kira catches my excitement-hysteria and also dresses up for the occasion. Chanti, two, is the only one who is calm. The thrills of Marine World are barely seen by Kira. "When is the plane coming, Mommy?" she asks. "When?" A real-live Granddaddy, far better than a dolphin, a dream coming into her world.

A half-hour before his plane is scheduled to arrive we are parked and entering the terminal. I stop at the desk to ask if the plane will arrive on time.

"The plane came in already," the man tells me. "It was an hour early. Winds."

My god, my Father is here and no one is there to meet him. He will get lost and wander off in San Francisco, and I will never see him again. He will be even more lost on the streets of San Francisco than on the streets of New York. I am feeling panicky. We got this far, how can we lose it all because of a damned wind?

There is my Father, right where he is supposed to be. He is sitting alone in the front row of empty seats by the gate number he should be at. Rows of chairs are behind him looking hollow. He seems lost, staring into space. Dressed well, in an expensive sport jacket, white shirt, navy blue pants: Danny's good taste. He is neither as thin nor as damaged as I had feared but he has an institutional look about him, as if he is bereft of color, a flatness about his face.

All these details I do not see until later. All I see is that he is here, the plane has not crashed, he has not wandered off, and he is really here.

I go over and I hug him. "Daddy." He looks at me somewhat confused, smiles. I think he recognizes me. I am beginning to cry and he seems to be aware of this and to respond some to my feelings.

I introduce the children and Kira looks at my Father excitedly, touches his arm, smiling. He smiles back. Chanti climbs on the railing. I tell my Father that Robert will meet us later, after work, and we get up to leave.

The stewardess comes over and asks if we are taking my Father with us. "Yes," I answer her, "he's my Father."

"What's wrong with him?" she asks, "Why did he need meet-and-assist service?"

"He's been in the hospital and needed help," I answer, mumbling, avoiding eye contact, avoiding questions, feeling vaguely at home with the strange occupation of hiding.

MOST OF THE time my Father sleeps. I am not sure what he is thinking or what he wants. He hardly speaks at all. It's like my childhood when he was depressed: coming home from school seeing my Father unkempt asleep on the living room couch. I feel again the bewilderment and frustration.

We have given my Father our room and we try to get him upstairs during some of his naps so that we are not too affected. My Father refuses to bathe or change his clothes by himself, but I have been warned of this and I try to deal with it somewhat. I decide it's easiest to ignore the cleanliness aspect and just help him change his clothes every three days or four days. Kira wonders why he wears the same clothes for so long. I lie to her: His clothes weren't dirty.

When he eats with us we see his jaw once in a while jolt and lock from what I now know is tardive dyskinesia. Surprisingly, Kira doesn't ask about it; some inherent instinct of kindness.

But some of the time my Father is here it is all right or even good. I take down my photo album of black and white pictures from three and four decades ago. My Father and Mother in their twenties, thirties, me as a child. My Father with his arm around me on a mer-ry-go-round horse; Mother in a calf-length flowered dress; Father in a jacket and hat with pinched-in sides. Here is Aunt Ruth with a rhinestone broach pinned on a jacket lapel, over her heavy breasts.

I await my Father's responses nervously, standing over his shoulder and he seems to respond. I show him the new albums of Kira and Chanti and he seems to respond to these, too.

I ask if he would like to know what has happened to Mother and he nods. I tell him that she remarried and then divorced but I spare him the details of the disaster. How Don, a hardened ex-sailor

Mother met when he picked up her furniture for the Salvation Army got her to marry him and fund his training to be a Science of Mind Minister. That soon after he got a church appointment he began an affair with a young woman in the congregation, which everyone except Mother knew about until someone finally told her, leaving her humiliated, her self-worth and bank account at zero.

"Mother is in California, Daddy. She moved here about a year ago, after the divorce."

He does not say anything.

"Would you like to see Mother?" I ask. He looks at me as if he figures I should decide.

"I don't know, Daddy. Do you want to?"

A shrug.

"Let's talk about it later," I tell him, feeling his tiredness, which I should have seen earlier. "Do you want to go upstairs now and rest?"

Looking relieved, he nods his head and begins to go into the family room. I redirect him upstairs to our bed and he falls heavily down on the quilt.

Later in the week Mother calls and asks me if my Father wants to meet with her. I ask him, and he says no. She says she will call again the next day. This time she wants to talk to my Father but he doesn't want to go to the phone.

"Do you want to talk to Mother or see her?" I ask him again. "I need to know."

Being an intermediary is getting me anxious. The idea of them meeting seems bizarre—Mother with her incessant chatter and my Father with his silence.

"No," he says, leaving me to transmit the message to Mother. My Father closes his eyes heavy with sleep and communicates neither with Mother nor me for the remainder of the day.

MY FATHER IS willing to see photographs of Mother with the children and home movies with her in them but I am finding out that in limited areas he is sure of what he wants and doesn't want, and contact with Mother is definitely not what he wants.

He agrees to go see the Mets play the Giants in San Francisco with Robert one day and silently seems to enjoy it. And he seems to like the children in a soft, gentle way, stroking their hair tenderly when they are near. He goes with us to the park by the river and we have an easy picnic on the grass.

All in all the ten days have gone by better than anyone expected, and while we wait at the airport for my Father's plane to New York to board I ask him if he has enjoyed being here. He offers a quiet smile and nods yes. And then I ask what I have to: "If it can be arranged—I don't know if it can, Daddy—but if it can . . . would you want to move here after the summer, if we can find a place for you to stay?"

"Here?" he asks.

"Yes. Move here."

"Yeah," he says, understanding, his face taking on expression.

"You think you would like it here?"

"Yeah. Yeah."

"Don't you think you would miss New York?"

"No."

"Aunt Ruth?"

"Uh uh."

"Danny?"

"No."

"You really want to live here if we can find a place for you?"

"Yes."

And so I am left to make or not make the next move.

WEEKS GO BY and life seems easy and routine most of the time. Today, here is Chanti, sweetness and joy in a butterfly painted shirt, watching Sesame Street. Robert and Kira are enjoying swimming at a club nearby, and I have a little free time which I am learning to live with.

But a few days ago I couldn't get a handle on my feelings.

Not enough sleep. And another painful cyst on my ovary. A big over-bloated plum on my right side stretching me from inside and pressing on my groin. I knew it was just a cyst that would go away on its own, like it did last time, but still fear began to take over. What if it was something serious?

I felt myself sliding, panicking, losing control. When I asked Kira to give Chanti some of her crayons she told me "No" and I yelled at her and gripped her shoulders hard to try to maintain my control. I turned on Kira without provocation, when we have been so close. Just the day before, snuggled in my arms, she said, "I would never want any Mommy but you, Mommy, I love you so much."

How I hated yelling, not just at her, but later at Chanti and Robert.

Later that evening, when we arrived at a restaurant we'd been wanting to try out, the atmosphere was loud, stuffy and chaotic. I escaped into the bathroom for a moment of peace and quiet. The bathroom was stark white except for a gray floor and gray baseboard all around the walls about six inches high. It was a small room, like a cell. There were only the white toilet, a tiny white sink, and a bare white bulb overhead. I fantasized locking the door and never going out. I started shaking. Panic consumed me. I felt trapped in a small gray and white institution and was sure I would never get out.

And then I caught myself reflected in the mirror. I looked like my Father: uncared for, depressed and institutionalized. Impoverished—the horrific word came to me. I wanted to run from the awful face I saw in the mirror but I couldn't look away. I looked like my Father, but much uglier, with my too-large mouth and irregular face, and without his silver-blue eyes. Lines, shadows intensified my defects in the strange light in the mirror from the bare bulb overhead. I am going crazy, I thought. I am on the irreversible road to insanity.

Water, I splash water on my face, sit down on the closed toilet seat and breathe slowly and regularly, in and out, remembering to make sure the breaths out are long enough so I don't add hyperventilation to the mess I am making of myself. And after a few minutes of self-inflicted agony, I open the door very slightly and see my family. Everyone has crayons and they are happily coloring on their placemats. No one looks afraid or angry or depressed. I am in a restaurant, not an institution.

I close the door, wipe my face, fix my hair, take good breaths and return to the table, grateful to have sanity to go to.

Again I wonder if my Father, when he was in his thirties, had had somewhere safe to go—someone to listen to him as Robert listened to me without judgment when we returned home—would he, too, have been able to return to his life? Would he be where he has been for so much of his life, in a place within a place, a room within a room, in white and gray walls in a small, closed-in space, without freedom, contact or care?

I shudder thinking of the conditions my Father has been in, the institutional life at River Court, where he may not even be able to remain with all the bureaucratic shifts. What will happen to him next? I make a solemn promise to move my Father to California. There is no other choice.

I join Robert, Kira and Chanti in decorating placemats, finding a red crayon and drawing a heart in the center. I will listen to my Father's heart and his presence when he is here, to his silence if he cannot speak. Perhaps I can share with him a small part of my developing strength.

WITH OTHER CHANGES in River Court, a new, harsher psychiatrist has been hired and my Father has been assigned to his care. His idea of care is to get him out of River Court into Brooklyn State Hospital. Unfortunately for him, fortunately for my Father, Brooklyn State Hospital has denied his petition to admit my Father, having determined that he does not have severe enough symptoms for hospitalization. The psychiatrist is exasperated because my Father refuses to take meds, medications which of course have never worked and torment him with their side effects. "Electric shock treatment would be my recommendation," he tells me.

And recent headlines in the papers have been exposing the horrors of mental hospitals: whippings, drug overdosing, filth, contamination, torture, strapping people down by the wrists and ankles indefinitely. Silencing with medication and shock. Silence. The silence unto death. No news to me. Just a reminder.

In an opinion piece, someone asks how we can close up in death wards such an enormous segment of the population because they appear to be different. He speaks of it as a tragic waste of human resources.

What will stop this psychiatrist from trying again to send my Father to Brooklyn State and eventually succeeding? I have to get my Father out of there and soon. I will use every resource I have to help him begin a new life and other people will help, too. I love my Father and I don't want him to return to the back ward of a hospital and live a living death. If I can prevent it.

I AM WAITING for a list of adult board and care homes to arrive so I can visit them and see if they would be suitable places for my Father to live. Perhaps I can find a "foster home" that boards only four or five people, where he will have his meals and a room of his own; a place where someone will help him gently change his clothes in the morning, take them off at night, encourage him to begin doing these things on his own. Perhaps I can even find someone to speak with him, as one individual to another. And we will be here for him, to make life a little easier, softer and lighter than it has been.

I almost look forward to checking out the facilities, to seeing if there is a place where my Father would be comfortable. I even fantasize asking the people at the corner grocery to give him a job for a few hours a week, not paying him, or even paying them something, so he will feel useful again and be in contact with people.

I used to worry about what Kira and Chanti would think of my Father, concerned about their knowing that they had a grandfather like him, but this dilemma doesn't seem real to me now.

On a TV talk show, Renee Richardson related a story as an answer to someone in the audience who wanted to know what affect her sex change was having on her then eight-year old son. She said that one time when her son was outside playing with the little girl down the block, thinking she would educate him, she asked him why he thought that although the girl was older than he was, she was shorter. Her son thought for a minute and then shrugged his shoulders. "I don't care why," he said. "It's *her* life."

To be accepting of others and to allow my Father to be who he is, regardless of other people's images and expectations. This is what I want to model and share with my children.

THREE MONTHS LATER we are at the airport again, this time well before my Father's plane comes in. When he arrives he looks almost cheerful and happy to be here in California and Robert and I carefully navigate us from the airport to the car. On the way home my Father sits in back with the children and, glancing through the rear-view mirror, I see him gently pat Kira's cheek with the back of his hand as he used to brush mine.

But as we arrive at our home, there is a grunting sound from the back seat and when I turn around I see that my Father has vomited all over the car and himself. Incredibly, the vomit has not gotten on the children.

I help him out of the car and look in his eyes and see the exhaustion and despair clearly burning at me.

"Are you all right?"

"No."

We try to figure out how to handle his getting changed and upstairs to our bedroom which he will have until we find a place for him to live. Robert takes care of Kira and Chanti, and brings the valise upstairs. My Father follows me up the stairs and starts to lie down on the bed with its old patchwork quilt of many colors and patterns that we found at an antique store several years ago.

"Daddy, wait. Get out of your wet clothes first," I say. "You have vomit on your shirt and pants."

He shakes his head. "It's okay," he mumbles, and begins to lie down.

"Daddy, you need to change," I say again. "I don't want vomit all over my quilt."

He begins to lie down anyway and I grab his arm firmly while I get an old blanket out of the closet and throw it over the patchwork quilt. He collapses in his wet clothing, exhausted, and falls asleep. This is 4:00 in the afternoon Sunday, and he does not awaken until I shake him at 11:00 Monday morning.

Not exactly as my fantasies would have had it. Such a waste of time, fantasies, if their purpose is the understanding of reality.

I DID NOT want to wake him up and take him from one depressing place to another, with hardly a break, but I didn't know what else to do.

Such a struggle, to visit the places, explain the differences, deal with traffic, sometimes with the kids, and fight his inertia and my own. The household is neglected, children neglected, Robert, my needs, even my Father's; all taking its toll and wearing us out.

After my Father is asleep, I tell Robert in despair, "Why am I doing this? He doesn't even care. He's never cared about me, never cared about anyone but himself, why should I struggle like this for him when if I fell dead in front of him, he wouldn't make a move to try to save me?" I know it is true. And yes, I know, he can't.

I'm sorry. Again. I do not mean to ask of my Father more than he can give.

I want him to talk, to share with me his thoughts and dreams, but I have to accept him as he is or there is no chance at all for this to work.

I pass a store window the next day and see a poster that leaves me breathless. I wish I had found it a week ago, when my Father first arrived. It would have made things easier on both of us. The poster states:

> *If you cannot understand my silence,*
> *You will not understand my words.*

I will try harder. My Father need not speak to me if he does not want to. Or if it is more than he can do.

M Y FATHER IS asleep in our bed. His arms are around his body, crossed tightly around his waist in the position of a person confined in a straightjacket. How many times did he fall asleep forced into that position?

The clay sculpture I made of him in a white shirt tied from behind, sitting comatose in a chair with wheels that cannot move, is hidden so my Father cannot see it. I called the sculpture *Fixed,* in my mind combining the definitions "mended" or "repaired," which clearly my Father had not been by those entrusted to repair him, and "fastened in a particular position so it cannot move."

Alternate definitions of fixed, like "incapable of being changed" and "made impotent, rigid or neutered," applied to my Father, made me feel sick.

I also found that "a fixed game is one that is dishonestly arranged" and "a fixed idea or opinion is one that doesn't change, though it may be wrong." To me, these fit the mental health system he had for so long been dragged and drugged through.

And last there was the verb "to fixate" and its definition, "to acquire an obsessive attachment to someone or something." Here I clearly saw myself, in relation to my Father.

It is almost noon, and I know I should wake my Father up. Instead, I turn away and walk down the stairs, quietly, soberly, alone.

GARDENIA BOARDING HOUSE. Not a bad name. Not a bad place, either, considering all the places my Father has been in the last thirty-three years. Just a mile away from us—walking distance, actually; drop-in distance. Not bad people, either. Bill and Lauren, an unpretentious, down-to-earth couple in their thirties are willing to take on my Father. Kathy, Lauren's sister, who helps out, has a sense of humor and seems as if she's been transported directly from New York: my Father's style.

Kathy is only thirty-four years old, pretty in spite of her weight. She suffered a stroke some years ago and is mostly recovered but retains the identification with the sick and helpless.

"Kathy looks like Aunt Ruth, doesn't she, Daddy?" I asked one day. She has deep, large dark eyes, high cheekbones and black hair like his sister's and probably his mother's were, with their Spanish ancestry.

"Y'know how I get him to take a bath?" Kathy says. "I tell him I'm gonna get in with him!" She puts her arm around my Father. He is fairly short and tends to stoop. She is a good five inches taller than he is and her bosom wide and loose in a sweater nuzzles his shoulder. "Do you like me, Sam? Huh?" she asks flirtatiously, harmlessly, and my Father cracks a small smile in spite of himself and responds with a barely audible, "Yeah."

After three weeks, I get a call from Lauren to tell me that for the first time since he moved there my Father cleaned up and changed his clothes almost completely by himself, and he'd stayed up till 11:00 p.m. Life is good.

"BUT WHY DOESN'T Grandpa talk?" Kira whispers, wondering why my Father won't answer her simple questions, will only look away, his eyes, once as radiant as hers, now gray-blue fog in his lost eyes. Her platinum blonde hair is parted into two ponytails that are decorated with blue, yellow and red shiny beads like jewels. Her bangs, that I realize I have cut too long at their sides, to compensate for Mother cutting mine too short, frame her eyes, innocent pieces of sky.

We are in the kitchen, the blue and gray tiles picking up the colors of eyes, mood, beads, sky, softs and hards and the silence of questions without answers.

I am tired of apologizing for my Father, who so often sits, with his head hanging down, on one end of the antique blue couch, our precious find at an auction before Kira was born. I am tired of explaining, over and over, things I will never understand.

"What kind of ice cream do you want?" I ask Kira and Chanti who has followed us into the kitchen and at three is still too young to be concerned about Grandpa. Chanti and Kira sit on the wood stools at the counter and watch me get the small glass dessert dishes down from the cabinet and find an ice cream scoop, pretending her question never happened.

"Is it because he's sad?" Kira asks somberly, not yet willing to take her full attention from her grandpa and pass it on to the ice cream.

"I think so, little one," I say, carefully, "He's been sad for a very long time. And there's nothing you did or can do that will change it. One day, when you're bigger, maybe twelve, I'll tell you more about Grandpa. But for now, what do you think? A little chocolate, vanilla and strawberry? I bet I can find some chocolate syrup to drizzle some hearts on top—Chanti—a little bit of each—or a lot?"

And we get down to the business at hand: filling fluted glass bowls with scoops of brown, white and pink, decorated with syrupy swirly hearts, the colors and flavors of the moment for the moment overriding the grayed-out blues of the past.

I MAKE AN appointment for my Father to be assessed by a psychiatrist who takes Medi-Cal, so we can get his records from New York and maybe get him some help.

Acutely anxious or depressed people are waiting to be seen by the doctor. After waiting for over an hour, the receptionist calls my Father's name and we go in.

I dislike the man on sight, with his knowing look, rings of sanity on his fat fingers.

Still, I am very polite. I give him my credentials, tell him some of my Father's history, and explain that we need to have his records in California in case any problems arise. He does not mind being guardian of my Father's papers and we have my Father silently sign a release so they can be sent.

I tell the psychiatrist that my latest concern is that my Father has been shoplifting small items at the supermarket even though he has money in his pocket and doesn't need to.

"Well, if he keeps that up, he may have to go to a locked facility," the psychiatrist tells me.

"He is doing fine except for this, and he should not be locked up just for taking a candy bar or a package of sliced ham. He doesn't understand he's not supposed to. He eats it in the store in front of everyone."

He nods, not saying anything. He stands up. No more questions. The interview is over.

I cannot resist. "Would you like to talk to my Father?" I ask.

The doctor hesitates. My Father is sitting in a chair looking dazed.

"No," he says. "I don't think that will be necessary."

No patient advocate, this man. What am I to do? There are too many crazies in the world for the doctors to even begin to understand or cope with.

A psychiatrist I see at a forum on mental illness says, "It is incredible the amount of humiliation schizophrenics have tolerated." Such a line, applying to all the mentally disturbed. "There is no single treatment for schizophrenia," he continues. "Patients are people first, and each person is unique and different." He describes schizophrenics as being in a state of "chronic delirium." I wonder how he would describe my Father's state when he is depressed: chronic death?

I think I will try this other psychiatrist who seems to care. After the lecture, he said I could bring my Father to see him.

But when I call, it turns out he uses a treatment called orthomolecular therapy and his fees are way beyond our means. "Sorry," the receptionist says. "The doctor does not see Medi-Cal patients."

WHAT WOULD MY Father say if he could speak, or write if he could write, about seeing Mother after all these years? I hardly have the words myself.

Mother lives in an apartment complex a few miles away, which makes it inevitable that she and my Father will meet at holidays and outings. Mother is good at grandmothering. She has patience with Kira and Chanti, playing Chutes and Ladders, Monopoly, Jenga and card games and she takes them swimming in the apartment complex's pool. She has strict orders not to force them to eat but by this time it isn't even an issue. We stock up her refrigerator with food they like.

Mother is prepared for her meeting with my Father, in her fashion, tidying up our family room when we come in from Gardenia House. My parents look at each other and think—what? She puts out her hand and they touch. She did not see him a half-hour ago, disheveled, dirty and unshaven, before we cleaned him up.

Mother asks him if he wants to go out with her to a restaurant, and he seems doubtful, checks me with his eyes for approval and I nod. He nods. What else am I to do, or he or she? Life is like that, small steps into what passes for reality. What could I have said to him before he left to make it easier?

Later Mother tells me that she told him why she had divorced him and he had seemed to listen. It sounds so pat, all figured out in tight, grammatical sentences, causes, effects, explanations. She had no choice, she told him. He was never willing to try. What could my Father respond to this, even if he could respond? Mother had common sense, eloquence, dignity and above all sanity on her side. There is no defense to a combination like that.

How could she wonder that my Father fell asleep when the two of them returned here?

"I think it was a little too much for him," she says to me, in the kitchen, worried.

I reassure her. "He is tired. That is all," I say.

"It's all right, isn't it?" she asks.

"Sure," I tell her. "I will take him home when he wakes up. Relax. I know it isn't easy for you. Not easy for any of us."

Christmas wasn't as bad. By this time Mother was just another disappointing ghost of the past. My Father seemed removed and tired. He wouldn't open most of his presents and hardly smiled at the ones the children made for him; and it's unlikely that he remembered the books we bought together to give to Kira and Chanti from him.

Part of the time he was alone in the living room resting on the couch. Mother saw him, walked in, and sat down on the rocker near him, beginning a stream of chatter.

I wonder what he could have been thinking, sitting silently, clearly out of place, listening to her words and her laughter chasing each other at breakneck speed as she told him one inane story after another, complete to the minutest most insignificant detail, about the inconsequential events of her life.

I should not presume, though, to read his mind. Perhaps he was not appalled as I was at her senseless barrage of words extinguishing silence. Maybe he was glad that she wanted to talk with him. Perhaps I am misreading the picture in his eyes; after all, he does not speak: how can I know?

Although she never finished the last of her story, and he never seemed to notice or care, as he came in for dinner and sat down, she following behind, losing their differences in blessed Silent Grace.

MY FATHER'S TEETH are invisible behind the thick layers of plaque. He has never been one to brush his teeth on a daily basis, but it appears he has not touched them with any implements at all in the past several years. Incredibly, his teeth are still set in his gums and he seems able to eat all right, the only disruption being the tardive dyskinesia spasming his jaw every once in a while. His mouth smells, though not as bad as you'd think—and I determine to have a dentist check them out.

I have taken my Father to three dentists for consultations. Each one looks uncomfortably and unenthusiastically at the putrid, foul smelling, thick crust of plaque that appears to be my Father's teeth from a safe distance and says with disgust the only option is to yank them all out. I respond to them with an equal amount of disgust that that is not an option.

And then we find Dr. Light, a periodontist nearby, who sets his chair close to my Father and actually looks carefully into his mouth, speaking to him with humanity and compassion, as if he is a person. He does not cringe when he looks in my Father's mouth. He does not have a pat, ready answer. He sits down and talks to us as if my Father and I are intelligent, feeling human beings.

"You have to look at the whole person," Dr. Light says to me in his office while my Father sits in the waiting room, a magazine in his hands. "He'll never be able to handle dentures because of his jaw movements, even if he wanted to and was able to put them in. He doesn't brush his own teeth, so it's not likely he'll follow through on denture care. I think the best thing to do is to clean the teeth he has . . . slowly, a few teeth at a time . . . and give him continuing care after that. Maybe every two or three months."

I listen suspiciously for sarcasm, contempt, but no, his voice is kindly and matter-of-fact. "Do you think it's possible?" I ask.

"I think it is," he says. "Shall we give it a go?" And, "Yes, of course our office accepts Medi-Cal."

Dr. Light works out a plan that will take minimum effort on my Father's part and mine, and he and the dental hygienist begin taking off at least twenty years of plaque and tartar, month by month by month.

Amazingly, the teeth buried underneath their plaque coating have not one cavity. Most are loose and wobbly—a couple almost fall out during the cleaning and have to be removed—but the rest are still functional.

Sometimes when I take my Father to Dr. Light for care I see severely damaged people in his office, and he and his staff always treat them with gentleness and never with any show of revulsion. One time a man with only half a face is waiting when we get there to see the hygienist. He looks as if one side of his face, including one eye, has actually been scooped out of his head. "Cancer," one of the staff tells me, shaking her head somberly.

And after almost a year of section by section scraping and cleaning my Father's mouth looks convincingly normal and the smell is more than tolerable, even at a close distance. Not that he ever brushes his teeth between his monthly cleanings. Not that anyone would expect him to.

YESTERDAY I CALLED my Father and told him I would pick him up to go to the park with us later that afternoon and asked him to please change his clothes. When I called Kathy to see if he was ready, she said he was still unclean, unshaven and unchanged. But later she calls and it seems her technique of teasing him that she'll get into the bath with him worked this time. My Father looks good when I arrive; he is clean and shaven, wearing a light blue shirt and beige pants.

The five of us go to the park by the river and throw a beach ball back and forth in the warm spring day. My Father's ability to throw and catch is still excellent, and he manages to participate more than he ever has. I'm not surprised that he still has bodily memory. When I took him bowling a few weeks ago, he threw a few balls and made strikes and spares, like he always had. Too bad he had zero cognitive understanding of the game or his ability. He never even smiled when all the pins went down.

I drop Robert, Kira and Chanti at the house and drive my Father back to Gardenia House. "Daddy," I say, when we arrive, "if I asked you to scale how happy you are on a scale of one to ten, how would you scale how you've been feeling?" First he says he doesn't understand, and I repeat the words, asking him to tell me which number comes to his mind. But I am unprepared for his answer.

"Nine," he tells me.

"Nine?" I ask. "Are you just saying that to get me off your back?"

My Father seems to appreciate my attempt at humor, but does not agree or disagree.

I walk him inside Gardenia House. We go into the kitchen where I pay for his room and board. Kathy chats about the simplicities of the day, starts to serve up meatloaf and homemade sliced boiled potatoes and peas. The house is warm, though untidy and not very clean. I ask if I can have a sample of the meatloaf and she gives my Father a taste, too. She winks at my Father and smiles. She tells him to take off his jacket and wait in the living room for a few minutes until dinner is called. The other boarders are in there and a couple wave to me on my way out.

Not what I would scale a nine, not at this point in time. But for my Father, compared to the places he has been and the treatment he has been subjected to, why not a nine? If he actually scales it a nine. If he even understood the question.

THE HEART-SHAPED Schrafft's or Whitman's Sampler boxes were usually red with gold lettering or with a big, red, satin bow across the center. Once there was a gold couple dancing on the lid like golden shadows and another time the hearts were dark burgundy with red flowers and lace around the edges.

When my Father was home, not in the hospital or too dazed to do anything, he would ceremoniously give us chocolate Valentine boxes, the large one with 25 chocolates separated in their fan papers for Mother and the matching small Valentine box, with only eight or ten chocolates, for me. It meant to me that my Father loved me as well as Mother, but safely, proportionately. We would spend hours at the kitchen table, with Mother cutting the chocolates into three even sections and distributing them. We would taste them slowly, comment on their individual flavors. My favorite was the coconut in dark chocolate and I was usually offered whole the cherry swirling in clear sugary fluid inside chocolate that would crack and slide slowly around my tongue and teeth until I chewed and licked it into oblivion. The memory of those chocolates tied me to my Father, demonstrated to me his generosity.

And today Kira, eight, and Chanti, five, sit with me at our family room counter, ready to glue heart-shaped white paper doilies onto red hearts cut from heavyweight papers. They have carefully drawn half-hearts along the fold. Kira cuts hers out by herself but I help Chanti, a lefty, who has a rough time cutting, since good lefty scissors are hard to find. And small hands, holding markers in every rainbow color, draw I love yous, arrows, flowers, butterflies, moons, stars, suns and trees, individualizing each Valentine's Day card.

I watch the depth of concentration. Chanti sucks on her bottom lip, Kira pushes her braids out of the way. Concentrate, concentrate. I love you Grandma. I love you Grandpa. I love you Gabrielle. I love you Marnie. I love you I love you I love you surrounds our pine table as the afternoon rides slowly on, a day with moments of simple, uninterruptable bliss.

I PICK UP my Father at Gardenia House to go to lunch with Mother, a commonplace event now that Mother has moved from her apartment a few miles away to a house we found for her around the corner. It is a true granny house, pale yellow, with a peaked roof and a fireplace, an entry window in which we have hung stained glass tulips in a round frame. It is across from a school, and Mother enjoys watching the junior high kids coming and going and when the track is deserted she does her daily one-mile walk around it. The Sacramento Natural Foods Coop and Taylor's Market are only a few blocks away, and Kira and Chanti can go over to her house after school and other than boundary issues—it is not okay for her to come over anytime without calling—it is working out well for all of us.

My Father is sitting on the couch at Gardenia House watching TV with two other disheveled men when I arrive and I go through the exhausting routine of helping him dress, which I do whenever Kathy is off work.

He seems even more somber than usual, though perhaps it is me, not him. In the car I ask if there is anything new and he shakes his head slightly.

"Ask me," I challenge.

He ignores me.

"Come on. Ask me if there's anything new." I persist.

Finally he repeats in a monotone, "Anything new."

I surprise him by answering, "Yes." I tell him about the wisdom tooth I recently had extracted.

"Let's see," he says and when we stop at a red light I let him search my mouth for the missing tooth. For a fragile moment, we are related, connected.

Encouraged, I begin to tell him that Chanti has lost another baby tooth, but my Father has shifted back to his own thoughts and does not respond.

In my mind I go over the scene from the evening before that I would have loved to share with my Father. Chanti had hidden her tooth in the heart-shaped tooth pillow that I sewed for her along with her hand scrawled note: *dear tooth fairy please leave me money but don't take my tooth.* I sang her a lullaby and tucked her and Raggedy Annie in. On cue, Kira, slender and delicate, in my long cream-colored silk slip with thin straps, blond hair loose and flowing, entered the edge of Chanti's room from the low-lit hallway. In an ephemeral, numinous, barely recognizable voice, she sang, *I am the tooth fairy . . . I have come to bring you a gift in exchange for your tooth . . . .* Chanti, barely awake, part of her knowing it was her sister but another part of her wanting the mystery, sighed in wonder as Kira gently slipped a quarter under her pillow without claiming her tooth and floated her way back out into the hall as I dimmed out the hall light.

Nor do I ever get to share with him how Kira at around the same age as Chanti told us one day that she knew who the tooth fairy was. "Who is the tooth fairy?" I asked her. "Grandma's daughter," she said, in a moment of clarity. And yet, when her next tooth fell out, she seemed to have no recollection of her revelation—hid her tooth under her pillow and was amazed when a quarter appeared in the morning.

My Father and I arrive at my house where Mother is waiting. She greets him: "Hi Sam. How are you?" He nods. Mother talks to me about the various restaurant possibilities as if it were crucial whether my Father prefers Chinese to Italian, steak and eggs to spaghetti.

Without responding, I steer them out the door as quickly and gracefully as I can.

MOTHER KNOCKS ON the door an hour later. When I
let them in, Mother leaves my Father standing in the hall
and rushes up the stairs, clutching her purse, like the White Rabbit clutching his pocket watch and says breathlessly, "I have to go
upstairs . . . can't talk about it now." She disappears from sight, leaving me confused, my Father drifting. By now I am as used to being
confused as my Father is to drifting.

"What happened, Daddy?" I ask.

"Nothing."

"Did Mom pee in her pants or something?"

My Father half-smiles and shrugs, sits down in the dining room
to skim through *Time.*

After a few minutes I go upstairs to talk to Mother. She is
extremely distressed.

"Some teenagers tried to rob me! A girl was the lookout—I knew
there was something wrong. It was my own fault. I was swinging my
purse and I know better than to hold it like that. You have to tuck it
under your arm or you're a sitting duck.

"These two boys came running toward me and I knew something was going to happen so I pulled my purse close and had a
tight grip on it. One of the boys grabbed at it and he yanked and
pulled but he didn't get it out of my hands. The other one came and
knocked me down! I hurt my back falling but he didn't get my bag
either. I started to scream as loud as I could and then they ran away.
I guess I was too much for them.

"But your Father—he just stood there and didn't lift a finger to
help me. When I finally got up he looked at me blankly and said,
'What happened?' I couldn't believe it!"

I guess it's true that if I collapsed in front of my Father he wouldn't do anything to help me. Is he indifferent or isn't he playing with a full deck? Or is his despair such that events like robbery, illness, and death have no meaning for him?

Or is it simply that he cannot understand (never could understand) the clinging to material possessions? Like anti-heroic characters, he possesses nothing that can be taken from him, not even his good name. He walks the streets in torn, soiled shirts, pants and coat, unlaced shoes, unshaven, ungroomed, with neither money, credit cards nor important papers in his possession. Mother, on the other hand, accumulates more of each of these and carries them close to her side.

Mother will never let go of her symbols of security without a struggle and a fight. My Father will drop even his body, and, in spite of his fears, never notice the impending or actual loss.

A UNITARIAN MINISTER shares his experiences at the podium. He has traveled all over the world and has seen the despair of people plagued by famine and fatigue. He talks of caring and equality and is absorbed, almost euphoric, in his convictions and commitment.

I could not take my eyes off this man. In some ways he could have been my Father's double: the same build, bone structure, deepened, expressive silver-blue eyes, same age. But the fervor and compassion in the words he spoke were in a different realm.

Heresy. I wish this man were my father. I wish I could hold onto him and lean on his strength and his kindness, be his child. I am torn with envy of his imagined children.

Sometimes I hear friends speak of their fathers. Usually I am silent and just listen, but if it is someone I trust or if I feel like gaining sympathy, I tell them some choice tidbit from my Father's life—a joke, a trespass, a disaster. I do not say that I lie in bed at night wishing guiltily that my Father were an alcoholic; it would be so much easier to explain his behavior if he were under the influence of something outside of his own self.

An acquaintance tells me that her father is a therapist in the Bay Area and she can get a job there partly because of his reputation. A friend's father goes around to different schools and churches by invitation, lecturing on Viktor Frankel's *Pursuit of Meaning* and teaching his theory of Logotherapy. I am so jealous I can hardly breathe.

What would it have been like to come from a home such as this? To have a set of grandparents for my children? A solid father, for me? To have never had this meaningless struggle?

Hush. He gave what he could, and it is all right.

I HAVE NEVER been introduced to the art of gingerbread house construction, but Robert has brought Christmas to our home and making gingerbread houses has become one of our traditions. The ritual lighting of the Menorah, Chanukah songs about dreidels and latkes with applesauce are no match for the extravaganza of Christmas. When I was a child, Christmas was something other people did, and its only meaning was the chance to get free candy and a coloring book if I waited on the long line in front of Macy's and didn't mind being a hypocrite to Santa Claus.

Now early in December we drive to the foothills and cut down a fir tree at a designated tree farm. We explore the woods, sometimes in the snow, Snoodles joyfully running around us. I obsess on finding the perfect tree to fit in front of our living room window, tiring everyone out and becoming the family joke. On Christmas Eves we attend the candlelight service at the Unitarian Church where we embrace the music and the reverence of passing a lit candle from one person to the next, symbolizing the power and connection of universal light and hope. When she is six, Kira leads the church from the center aisle in "Let There Be Peace On Earth," and this is one of the experiences that lead her into studying theater.

The day before the Christmas Kira and Chanti are nine and six, instead of making gingerbread houses out of small milk containers and graham crackers as we have in the past, I make gingerbread dough from scratch so we can create our own unique versions of gingerbread houses. I buy ginger, cloves and molasses to add to the flour, baking soda, brown sugar, butter and cinnamon that I have at home, and the standard candy fare of gum drops, jelly beans, good and plenty, marshmallows, chocolate chips, and candy canes.

While the children are at their friends' house, I combine ingredients and roll out the dough, making enough for my project with plenty left over for Robert and the children to create their own experimental houses when they get home.

I pattern and carefully cut out walls and roofs to create a close replica of our two-story picture book house, with its three oddly-connected angled roofs, large half-dome front window, two brick chimneys. I cut out windows and open doorways and frost together a fanciful two-story 1927 home. I add decorative candies and place the completed house on a platter covered with frosting snow. It is a long day's labor of love.

The rest of my family stake out their ingredients that evening and we have, besides sticky fingers and mouths, four precious creations to grace the dining room for Christmas dinner the next day.

At 2:00 Mother arrives and I leave to get my Father from Gardenia House. He seems to be in one of his more cooperative moods and Kathy has been able to get him changed and looking almost normal. I find his coat and help him on with it. "A very merry Christmas to you," Kathy calls out as we walk toward the car in the cold winter air.

This is a good day. We walk into the house to the sweet scents of rosemary, cinnamon and nutmeg greeting us. Mother is easy with Kira and Chanti, Robert feels festive and enthusiastic, and I don't mind bringing my Father home. I finish last-minute preparations while the rest of our small family finds its way to the dining room table.

And the evening goes well. Everyone is relatively content with their presents and my Father barely awake but hanging in holds up his new light blue shirts and box of Sees candy for a photo.

It's not till after Robert takes my Father and Mother back to their respective homes and I am cleaning up that I notice that a big chunk of the front roof and the corner of the second story of my gingerbread house is missing.

There is no point in confronting the obvious perpetrator, my Father. Too much of him is missing to understand the difference between dessert—the two slices of pumpkin pie with ice cream that he has eaten—and my carefully crafted work of art. I try to laugh it off, after the initial shock. It's not that weird for him to want to taste it. It is made of gingerbread and candy.

And here it is, yet another chance for me to learn my lesson to let go of expectations.

I look again at the awkward structure and this time I realize I am staring into a metaphor: the gingerbread house is now like my Father—pieces are missing from the upper front end; the rest of it is relatively intact.

IT IS 6:30 and the phone rings, interrupting our dinner. It is Lauren. "Bill wanted me to call you and tell you what your Father did tonight."

I take a deep breath. "What happened?"

"Well, tonight we were serving ham, potatoes and broccoli for dinner—and the rule is that before you can have seconds you have to clear everything on your plate. I know Sam doesn't like vegetables, and I hardly give him any in the first place. He could finish them up if he wasn't so stubborn. Well, Sam wanted more ham when I came around with it, but he hadn't eaten his potatoes or his broccoli. So I told him, 'Sam, you can't have any more meat until you finish your vegetables.'

"Then I turned around to give someone else more ham—and no sooner was my back turned than Sam slid the broccoli and potato on the floor and walked out.

"We can't have that going on here. I have six people to take care of and I can't afford to feed them just meat. If he doesn't want to eat vegetables, that's up to him, but he can't go around throwing things on the floor."

I try to listen and deal with her feelings before I deal with my Father's, not to mention mine. "Sounds like you've been having a rough time of it," I say lamely.

"Damned right I have. I made Sam get back in, get down on the floor and clean up his mess. Bill told him we were gonna call you and he shook his head no but Bill wanted me to call so here I am."

Great. Here she is. "Do you want me to come over and talk to him?" I ask.

"No, he's right here. Just talk to him over the phone. Tell him he can't go on doing things like that. Tell him that you're ashamed of him for it."

Ashamed of my Father for what? For wanting to choose his own foods? When he used to protect me from Mother's controlling my food intake when I was a child?

My Father comes to the phone. He says hello and his voice sounds little and scared like a child's. What can I say? I ramble on about following the rules and not upsetting Lauren and Bill, about doing what he's told so he can stay at this place which is the best we could find.

I don't think he's even listening. When I ask him what he thinks I get a distracted "Yeah, okay." I hang up the phone, feeling sick about both of us.

I hope this does not become a continuing problem. I understand that my Father is hungry by dinner time. He doesn't wake up until after breakfast and doesn't like soup and sandwiches for lunch. But he could eat a vegetable or two and be gracious about it; it wouldn't kill him. And if he can't eat it, he can at least not throw it on the floor.

If he would take care of himself and change his own clothing, he could live in a rooming house instead of board and care and eat at whatever restaurant he wanted. He could eat meat at every meal. It's his own fault he's in this situation. Whatever that means.

AND TODAY THINGS are even worse. It is 3:00 in the afternoon and I am in the family room preparing to teach a parenting class that evening, when I get another call from Lauren. "I hate to have to tell you this, but two of the guys here saw your father pee on the tree next door. The neighbors complained about it, too." Clearly confused and uncomfortable, Lauren this time doesn't add to everyone's misery by putting my Father on the phone so I can shame him; she hangs up.

Should I not be shocked? Should I have expected this? Well, I didn't expect it. It is way beyond my fantasies.

Father, you cannot go around ignoring basic sanitary and privacy codes. You have to do some minimal things, whether they seem meaningful to you or not. You have to help Lauren dress you and shave you, not resist and stall and pretend you do not understand what she wants. You can't begin to shave and stop after a few strokes and say that is good enough.

And you cannot go outside and pee on the trees like a homeless person or an animal. Father, do you understand, this place is good. The people are fair, the other residents are trying, and this is a place you can live a good life in and call home. Father, please. I cannot give you the energy or the will. Please, somehow, from someplace, evoke your own.

I try to get back to what I was doing before the phone call. What was it? Oh, I remember—preparing to teach a parenting class tonight. Right.

Unsent And Unsaid

Why don't you go somewhere and die?
Do you think I like wanting to say that to you?
Feeling that for you?
How can you stay so long without caring?
I am afraid to be with you.
I am afraid you are contagious.
The disease of despair will infect me, infect us all.
I too despair, Father.
But I hope, too.

Father, Kira no longer greets you at the door.
She says you don't notice her anyway;
Or care.
I ask her to try,
But she is her own person.
I cannot make her care.

You can, Father, by caring for her.
You can make me care again, by caring for me.
You can make yourself care, by caring for you.

I do not want you to die, Father,
But it is too painful to watch you
In this despair:
Death layered over life.

I T BEGINS AS a routine trip to our home from Gardenia House, so my Father can fry up some eggs and flip them in the air sunny side over, which his body somehow, like bowling strikes, sometimes remembers how to do; and to hang out and look through magazines.

At the intersection of Broadway and Freeport Blvd there is chaos.

A heavyset woman is lying on her side in the street by a vehicle with its windshield crystallized. Her hand is on her head, which is spouting blood like a geyser. We are close enough to hear her screaming, "Oh my God oh my God oh my God," as she realizes that spurts of blood are pouring down over her face. Her small son, held in the arms of a bystander, is screaming, "Mama Mama Mama Mama Mama!!!!" Everyone else seems frozen, a still frame in an insane movie. All of us are helplessly watching this woman bleed to death.

I want to stop and see if I can help, but there is nothing I can do, there is already too much confusion. I can call the police, ambulance, and fire department from home, two minutes away.

My Father has been sitting next to me watching this gory scene and I momentarily feel panicked. The deaths of his parents, his fears of dying, his own brushes with death—who knows what might be dredged up from his past?

"Are you all right?" I ask, as I weave our way home. As usual, I am numb to my own feelings that I cannot afford to succumb to, although I see that my hands are trembling. My Father nods his head and seems to be all right. I wonder if he understood what happened.

I call the fire department as soon as I walk in the door (faster than 911 in emergencies) and am relieved to hear that an ambulance is already on the scene.

I never hear or read anything about the accident. Perhaps the woman made it after all—open head wounds are better than closed.

I wonder how a child can survive witnessing his parent's death in such a horrible way. At least my Father was not at the scene when his parents died. He should be grateful, I guess.

It does not occur to me till days later that my Father daily wanders the highly trafficked area near the accident and pays little attention to street lights, crosswalks, or traffic; and the bloodbath could as easily have been his. His and mine.

I TAKE OUT the old album of photographs and my Father and I look through some pictures. I stop at the wedding picture of my parents in sepia tones, the lace of Mother's dress swirling down the photograph, her smile guarded and mature; my Father's face boyish and shining as he smiles into the camera.

"Who's that?" I nudge my Father, playfully, pointing to him in the photo. My Father looks at the picture, then at me, and shrugs his shoulders. He is apparently confused.

"That's you," I tell him, confused myself.

He shakes his head.

"Do you know who that is?" I ask, pointing to Mother.

Another head shake.

"Daddy, you remember getting married, don't you? 1941? New York?"

My Father shakes his head. Negative.

"You're sure you don't remember anything?"

My Father is blank.

"You know that you were married, though, right?" I ask, feeling more and more off balance.

"No," my Father states. "I wasn't."

"Well," I say, figuring I hold the trump card, "If you were never married, then who am I?"

A shrug, a detached voice, "I don't know."

"You know I'm your daughter, right?" I say.

"I don't have a daughter," my Father says unequivocally, reporting a simple unastonishing fact.

I am feeling a little bit crazy. "Let's look at some more pictures, Daddy," I say. Perhaps more recent ones will be recognizable. But my

Father admits to knowing no one, to recognizing nothing.

We come across a picture of my Father on a horse. I am standing nearby, probably eight years old. I tell my Father that the man in the photograph is him. He looks at the picture, then at me, and says with what is almost a smile, "Which one is the horse?"

I can't figure out what in the world happened. Did my Father's memory just kick in and offer a joke he used to tell and if so why now?

The pervasive question continues to haunt me—not "Which one is the horse?" that I can answer; the cryptic question "Which incarnation is my Father?" that I cannot.

I AM IN touch with the extreme effort it takes my Father just to survive, to make the motions of even getting himself out of bed.

Usually I get irritated at him for not appreciating my efforts to draw him out, but now Iperceive it is his gift to me to be with me as much as he is.

Kathy tells me my Father is lying in bed with his eyes open but will not come to the phone or respond to her, although I hear her repeat "Your daughter's coming to see you," on the other end of the line. She is upset by his immobility and doesn't know what is going on.

I have seen my Father semi-comatose before. As if the experience helps.

The thought comes from nowhere. Perhaps he is dead and that is why he is lying there with his eyes open. That is why he does not respond.

I think, as I get in the car, prepared for the worst, that it's possible that I will now have to face my Father's death.

But my Father is not dead on arrival. He is sitting up in a chair in the living room, waiting. He does not even seem more depressed than usual.

All my preparation for nothing; big surprise.

He has not changed his clothing, won't change when Kathy asks him to anymore, even when she makes her old attempts at beguiling him into nudity. I take him back to his room to go through the formidable task of having him change. But one thing has come out of this. For some reason, I have become more sensitized to the effort everything is for him.

"Daddy," I say, when we get into his room, "I want you to know that I appreciate your changing your clothing. I know it's something you would rather not do, and that you do it only for me."

My Father meets my eyes and nods slightly, then with some energy begins getting dressed, so we can go out together for lunch, leaving me more confused than ever about what goes on in my Father's tenuous world.

IT IS THE MIDDLE of the night and I am unable to sleep. My throat is sore and it is hot in the room and I am oppressed with tangled thoughts. Robert wakes up next to me and offers to make us some warm milk with chocolate liqueur to soothe us back to sleep as he did on nights when I was pregnant and later when the children were up in the night, nursing.

I am preoccupied with plans for the next day coming rapidly at us when he returns with the warm drinks. Robert is supposed to take my Father and the children to see *Star Wars* which we missed the first time around, leaving me to have a free day. It has occured to me, in the middle of the night, that perhaps the movie will be violent. Too violent for Chanti, age seven? For my Father . . . age unknown?

"Robert, do you think you should take Sam to *Star Wars* or is it too violent?" I ask.

"Do you think Tolstoy should be put in Siberia or is it too cold?" Robert responds.

"That's not the same kind of question!" I lash out. I am furious that Robert is making a mockery of my Father and me and I am quick to protect us both. But in a minute I cannot help myself and I begin to laugh. Who knows? Maybe it is the same kind of question.

It has been several years since my Father has been high and he may be due for another breakdown, I muse, warm milk and liqueur beginning to take effect. There's been so much memory loss, though, it almost seems it would interfere with a manic cycle, as shock treatments do, cutting out unwanted material and creating a bland silence.

Is a person the same person if his memory has had holes punched in it? Does it matter how many, how large, how contiguous; shape, uniformity, or location; what area of the brain? Or is memory a part of a person at all?

Mercifully, my own mind weakens as I succumb to a liqueur-induced temporary memory loss of my own, and drift into an uncertain, much needed sleep.

I AM TALKING to a friend on the phone and the operator interrupts: "Emergency call for you, from Kathy. She's on the line and says she has to talk to you, so you must hang up."

An emergency. Oh my god. Now what.

"Well," Kathy says, in her slow voice. "It's not really an emergency. I couldn't get through the line for a long time so I had the operator interrupt. It's just that your dad won't take his bath and he smells so bad that no one wants to sit near him and they're making fun of him. I can't get him in, he won't listen to me, so I thought maybe you would talk to him and tell him to get in the tub."

Just a bath. No crisis. No sirens in the night, glazed eyes, unspent energy, depression unto death. Just a simple bath problem. But how simple? I talk to my Father on the telephone and explain that he has to take a bath because he smells bad. I tell him I will be seeing him tomorrow to take him to a Japanese food fair in the area. "Will you take the bath?" I ask.

"Okay," he says.

"Now?"

"Yeah."

Relief. A crisis averted. But a half hour later my suspicions are aroused. I call back.

"No, he refused to go in. And I am afraid someone is going to get really angry and hit him he smells so bad."

I feel impotent. It is not a private issue when he smells so bad he offends everyone around him.

"I will be over in a few minutes," I tell Kathy. "Perhaps together we can talk him into getting into the tub."

I watch through the door slot
As my Father stands naked his
       back towards me,
Scratching his backside
Deciding if he

Should would could
Go into the bathtub
I have cleaned and refilled with
       warm water.

My Father doesn't like baths.
Or showers.
But he is beginning to smell more than
       even his world will take,
So I am helping him survive in this element
I think.

Put your foot in, Daddy.
I will

No water sounds.

Daddy, I can't hear any splashes.
Nothing.

Daddy.

Water sounds.
Light sounds. One foot. The other.

Relief floods me. No confrontation.
This time.

I wait.
I sit on his bed and I wait.

My Father is out.
I look him in the eye.
He looks back, poker faced.
He is the master at control, I a neophyte.

Daddy, you have put your dirty clothing
           back on.
What?
I lead him back into the bathroom.
Show him his clean clothing
In a while he comes out with his shirt changed over
           the dirty underwear.

Listen Daddy it is hot I am tired go on in
           now and change it all everything.
I changed my shirt
I can see that Daddy, but one card does not a deck make.
Humor, the ace.
But are we playing with a full deck?

I walk into the hot room with my Father and he changes his
           undershirt, slowly puts back his clean shirt.
I leave as he begins to change his undershorts
And return to see that he has also put on his new pants.
I pass him his belt.

The clean socks are still hanging on the edge
      of the toilet.

All right, Daddy. That's enough.
We go into his room and I get his razor set up.
He shaves leaving sections unclipped
      beneath his chin.

We walk out and head for the car.
We will silently go out for lunch,
      vaguely unified.

On the way it occurs to me:
I bet my Father never put more than his feet
      in the warm water.

HOW MUCH OF our few hours of life do we need to spend on the dead or unreachable?

While my Father is here in body only, my children are fully involved, body, heart, spirit and mind, in the exciting challenges that every day brings—the small stuff that makes up their days.

I watch Chanti, nine years old, do her homework and a few chores without prodding. I see her pattern and model after me, Robert, Kira, teachers and friends, trying to figure out how to navigate her world.

I wonder if she even thinks about this grandfather who for the past eight years is with us most Thanksgivings, Christmases and once in a while when she comes home from school. She never says. I never directly ask.

She is dealing with the day-to-day mysteries and challenges of growing up. When a friend in her class turns on her and says she's weird and others defect to her friend's side, we sit close on the soft mauve sofa by the glass doors in the family room. I can see dozens of oranges bending the boughs on the twenty-year-old tree and the camellias opening their red and white blossoms as I listen to her story. We wonder together how you stop kids from teasing you, making your life a temporary hell. I try to imagine my parents sitting down with me to help me figure out how to handle anything and come up with a big blank. They had no time, no skills, no consciousness and were too self-absorbed to notice my unhappiness. And their own parents offered them even less.

Chanti has begun crying. It's been a long time since she was picked on; the last time was when she was in kindergarten, ridiculed for sucking her thumb. It wasn't even by the children—it was the bus driver who dared to humiliate her, asking her if she wore diapers, getting a laugh from the bigger kids on the bus. The next day I was at the bus stop letting him know if he ever, ever said one rude word to her again he'd be out of a job and I made sure she got an apology. Again I wonder, who stood up for me? Who stood up for Mother, only seven, on her first day at school in England, having a few days before arrived from Poland speaking only Yiddish, her head shaved by immigration to check for lice since it was too much trouble to check for lice in pale blond hair. Who stood up for my Father, no parents to go to for anything after he was ten.

Chanti and I do some problem solving, the kind I have been teaching since before she was born, a gentle system for solving problems creatively. We have used this technique together usually successfully since she was two and we worked out how to solve the problem I had with her getting white glue on the carpet when she was experimenting with her art supplies and she was adamant that she wanted to use the glue whenever she felt like it.

"Chanti, it's hard for Mommy to get the glue off the carpet. And I know when you have it it's hard not to sometimes spill some when I'm not helping you. Can we try to find a way that we can both win?"

After several ideas that neither of us can live with:

"Hide it," Chanti offers.

"Hide the glue?"

"Yes. So you can help me when I need it."

"I can get it for you when you need it?"

"Uh huh."

And now we brainstorm ways to handle a more intricate problem: how to protect one's self-esteem, so much more tender than white glue or a carpet. And after several ideas, some far less elegant than others, about what to do or say if she gets called weird again, Chanti settles on saying a cool "Thank you" and moving on to do something else. How smoothly this works, as her friends are quickly bored when she doesn't react, teaching her at a still young age lessons about avoiding the role of victim. And, remembering how bad it feels to be laughed at, she knows she would never be part of the bullying crowd.

Kira, too, has had to figure out ways to survive school. When she started pre-school at three years old, Jill, one of the older kids, age four, started calling her a baby, leaving her upset and isolated. After listening for a while, we began problem solving and we brainstormed together how she could handle Jill.

We listed several solutions that seemed like good ones: invite Jill over and become friends; talk to the teacher; talk to Jill's mother; ignore Jill and play with other kids; I could come to school and help them work things out; and some we had to cross out as not acceptable options, like "kill Jill," but then Kira thought up her own innovative solution.

"I should tell Jill to call my baby sister a baby, not me," she said, thinking of Chanti just turned six months.

"Hmmm," I said, nervously, "Do you think Jill would really listen to you? Maybe it would be easier if you invited her here and said it."

"It's okay, Mommy," Kira said. "I think I've got it solved."

And the next day I didn't hear any complaints about Jill. And when I finally asked Kira what happened she said off-handedly, "Well, I told Jill to call Chanti a baby, not me, and Jill said, 'Okay.'"

I wish I could problem solve away my problems with my Father. Unfortunately for me and for him, he isn't able to have a conversation. And it's hard to problem solve when the other person can't articulate or understand what anyone wants or needs. I don't want to think about my Father. I want my attention to be with my children, with the present and future, not the past. I know it's selfish but I just want to listen to my daughters' small and big stuff. I just want to listen to my own.

I AM USED to Gardenia House after almost ten years, and feel relieved that my Father has a stable place to stay and other people to look after him. It isn't the best environment, of course, but then my Father isn't exactly the perfect resident. They have been willing to put up with him, with his constant mouth and body odors from never brushing his teeth and rarely bathing, with his occasional smearing his feces on the wall in the bathroom, his pile of boogers texturing the wall by his bed. And they have several times recently picked him up at the local market before the police hauled him away for gulping milk out of the cartons and tearing ham out of the plastic casing and eating it on site. And while they have not suffered in silence, they have allowed him to stay. They have even, at times, been amused by his eccentricities.

So it is a shock to me when I get a call from the Sheriff's Department telling me that Sam Levy—is he related to you?—is being held in custody because the couple running Gardenia House have been taking their charges' social security checks and starving the residents. "Lots of bills from drugs and gambling," the man on the line informs me. "This one guy," he says in disgust, "is 6' 2" and weighs 124 pounds. Nothing but skin and bones, poor critter." I mentally identify Charlie, one of several other men who have shared Gardenia House with my Father for the past few years. Charlie, quiet, gentle, uncomplaining, who sometimes helped convince my Father to get bathed and dressed, simply by virtue of his size. The men tended to be cooperative with him, as Lauren said. He'd weighed a lot more than 124 pounds the last time I'd seen him. But I hadn't seen him, for months, I realize when I think about it. "But my dad wasn't that thin when I saw him two or three weeks ago," I mumble. "No," the man says. "He's not that thin. Might have lost a little weight since you saw him, but he's not emaciated or anything. He's the only one though. The only one with relatives."

What am I to do with my Father now? There aren't a lot of places that can deal with someone like him. Someone like him.

The men, including my Father, are given temporary shelter overnight, and the next day we again begin our exhausting journey from one possible placement to another, to find a place that's acceptable to me; a place that he's acceptable to. The other men, lost souls in an anonymous, inadequate healthcare system, are not my problem.

I think about Dorothy Puente, who only a few miles away murdered the residents of her board and care home and buried them in her backyard. I wonder if we stopped at her place when my Father first arrived. I feel myself trembling with revulsion. He could have been buried by now as the others had been. No, he would not have; the boarders she took in had no relatives.

There, I am of some use after all. At least I keep my Father alive and I keep him from being starved to death. Suddenly it occurs to me that maybe the reason he was stealing from the market was that they weren't feeding him much at Gardenia House. Maybe he wasn't doing it just because he was deranged. Maybe he was taking food because he was hungry.

MY FATHER LOOKS frightened when I pick him up, and yes, he has lost some weight. I think guiltily that he must have lost some of it the last time I saw him but I hadn't noticed. We go from place to place, tired, hot, the stench from my Father's mouth and body at times overwhelming me, and making me feel that anyplace would be okay, if he is just somewhere out of the range of my breath. I'm not even sure why I am taking him with me. He doesn't care where he lives.

I finally find a board and care home that seems lovely—too good to be true, and as it turns out, it is. It is near my house and the two people who are running it seem willing to work with my Father. Of course they don't know all the details of his history. Mostly they know that he'd been abused at this last home, and so they feel sorry for him. They don't have many people there and he obviously doesn't talk much, so he seems like a bargain. Yes, they'll help him bathe and dress, and even let him make a sandwich in the kitchen if he wants to.

I feel a renewed commitment to my Father's care. Maybe, maybe we can pull it off. It's so close to our home—only a couple of minutes away— maybe he can be part of our family more often.

It works okay for about two weeks. Then the complaints start coming in. "I just asked him to bring his plate to the kitchen and he refused to do it," comes the voice at the end of the phone. My stomach tightens.

"He doesn't understand," I try to explain to her. "He's got pieces missing in his head. Things don't compute right."

"Well, he's just refusing. I think he understands perfectly well. He just won't do what he's told."

The beginning of the end, of this episode at least. It goes from bad to horrendous. One day it is not bringing his plate in, the next it is finding pee spots in the corner of the bedroom carpeting. Now the formerly sweet, accepting woman is outraged. "Who's going to pay for this damage? Who? Are you?" Well, yes, me, I agree and hand her a twenty-dollar bill.

But the writing is on the wall, hieroglyphics crayoned in fact, in brown smelly handprints all over the bathroom walls. My Father passes the last boundary of civilization and smears his message of profanity on polite society where, as they let me know in no uncertain terms, cleanliness is next to godliness.

I go over to the house as quickly as I can and the woman is enraged. "Come up here and look," she yells at me. "Just look at what he's done." She drags me upstairs and points at my Father as if she is pointing to dog shit on the rug. "Look what he's done," she screams shrilly. "What kind of an animal is he? Your Father is disgusting, he's disgusting."

My Father is cowering, confused. "How can you be such a disgusting pig?" she attacks, turning to him. "Here, you clean it up," she screams in his face, handing him a wet rag. "Here you filthy animal. You clean it up. Do you think I'm a slave to clean up your shit?"

She is on a rampage and I can feel shame and rage pounding in my throat. My hands are shaking and I look at my Father's frightened, uncomprehending eyes and try to defend him. "He doesn't understand," I tell her. "Leave him alone. He doesn't understand."

But she does not stop. She sticks the rag into his hand, turns him around and tries to pull him over to the wall covered with smeared brown smelly scrawlings. He pulls his arm away and I tell her to leave him, leave us, alone. I lead him as quickly as I can down the stairs to the sound of her tormenting screams. "Disgusting animal. What kind of a human being . . ."

And back to my home where my Father collapses on my bed in exhaustion and I try to catch my breath and stop trembling and succeed for a while. Then I go downstairs and break down sobbing in great heaves of impotent, unyielding, shame, pity and rage.

THE NEXT DAY I add assisted living places to board and care homes. One medium-size place we visit seems possible. The staff is kind and not too put off by my Father. No, occasional peeing on the floor isn't a problem (incontinence, they call peeing on the floor). They have linoleum floors and walls that wipe clean easily. There are some people with beginning Altzheimers, and they assume that my Father's problem is dementia. Maybe it is, I think, hopeful that maybe there is a logical explanation for his actions, and it has been missed.

I visit my Father over the next few months in the gray somber room he shares with a man who talks to himself. My Father doesn't smear his feces on the walls or if he does no one tells me about it. Peeing in the corner of the bathroom or missing the toilet seat doesn't upset anyone much, and it is actually comforting to me to smell pee mixed with Lysol in the halls because it means that my Father may be able to remain at this level of care and out of total care—a nursing home or a locked facility.

My Father loses this placement after about eight months. He has been spitting in the halls, they inform me, and the spit on the linoleum is slippery, making it dangerous for the other residents who are walking, sometimes with canes or walkers, sometimes alone. He needs to stop spitting, they tell me. He can't do that here. I buy him handkerchiefs, tissues, a small washcloth, put them in his shirt pocket, in his pants, in his hands, but for the most part they go unused. Day after day I threaten, cajole and plead with my Father to stop spitting in the halls, explaining in as many ways as I can invent that it is dangerous for other people and that he will not be able to stay there if he doesn't stop spitting on the floors. But spit he will, and will again, regardless of what anyone tells him or the reasonableness of the request.

I go to meetings with the director and the staff. It's not that he's been any trouble any other way, they say, at first kindly. We're trying to give him time to understand. But gradually there is less patience, less understanding in their voices. The bottom line is they can get sued if someone else falls and breaks a hip.

What is there to say? They are right, of course. I can see that. Other people have rights and needs and by persisting in spitting in the halls he is what he never was before: dangerous.

My Father's pained silver-blue eyes do not count to anyone but me and even I have to forcibly push myself to remember the warm protecting arms, the gentle humor, the young man who could always carry a tune and patiently taught me over and over to almost carry one, too, who protected me through the crowds at Nathan's and Times Square. It is an effort to flash back to the pain and despair of someone in his thirties who was unable to find a place in this world. Even I have to convince myself to advocate for this person in front of me now, who is barely there.

"Not for this earth," someone said about my Father. But if not on earth, where?

Still I buy time, ignoring the welfare of other people's parents and grandparents, placed in jeopardy because of my Father, and me. I am afraid I will never be able to find an appropriate placement for an inappropriate person. I am afraid to go down another list of places from too horrible to too pleasant and the enormous range in between and to see all the disintegrating people cared for by tired, cheerless staff. I don't want to walk the streets, again, my Father meekly by my side, drooling now at the mouth, and locking his jaw and tongue as he tries unsuccessfully to speak an occasional word or phrase.

And in the end I receive a 30-day eviction notice, signed and notarized. And whether my Father or I can or can't go through with another search for a place for him to live is no one's concern but mine.

I AM TRULY grateful for Mary's Elderly Board and Care, not too far away from our home. It is another small place, but the people running it are not there to keep the place immaculate or to teach the residents manners. The only common area that can be walked through is the small foyer going from the living room to the bedrooms and it's carpeted; no hall with a linoleum floor to walk and spit on.

I explain as much of my Father's problems as I can to Mary, an elderly woman with broken English and her son, in his thirties. I try to walk the thin line between making them want to take him and giving them the information they need to decide if they can handle him. Eduardo, who does most of the work with the residents, seems good humored, full of energy and not afraid to help my Father. He doesn't think spitting will be a problem, since there aren't a lot of walking places and they will make tissues or a towel available for him. Incontinence, as they too call peeing on the carpet, isn't a problem either and I don't mention the smearing since it hasn't happened for several months. Bathing and changing him is not a problem either; they help one of the other men and they will be happy to do it for my Father. He can have his own room and the brown, flowered bedspread and orange mini-blinds with gauze orange curtains look kind of like a friendly, economy-priced motel. I notice a wooden bowl of fruit in front of the television and another bowl of candy and nuts. "Your dad can take whatever he wants," Eduardo tells me. "We like people to feel at home here." Mary smiles and nods accommodatingly.

They are so warm and engaging I can hear myself let out a breath of relief and hope.

And Mary and Eduardo are in fact what they seem to be: genuinely accepting, kind people. For several months, to my relief, my Father does better in this gentle environment than he has in any other since he arrived in California.

MARY CALLS AT 9:00 a.m. and tells me in broken English that I have to come over right away. "Serious," I finally make out from her accent. "No, no, can't wait till tomorrow."

I am about to drive to San Francisco to see the ballet with a friend, but ballet is suddenly far away and it seems absurd to think I can be a normal person going to a ballet.

When I arrive at Mary's, annoyed and anxious, I am taken to my Father's room. I stare at him from the safety of the doorway.

My Father is lying on his bed rolling rigidly from side to side in a sweat, his jaw clenching and locking. His sheets and blanket are halfway on the floor. He is digging his left hand which is in a fist into his head and face in a compulsive movement ending in his left eye which has become a thick, red, swollen mess. I am frozen except for the revulsion in my stomach and mouth. Mary points to the gauze orange curtains, which are shoved into the wastebasket near my Father's bed. "He took it down in the night," she says. "This too." She is referring to the metal blind I now notice hanging weirdly in front of the window. "He did that," she says. The left side of the blind has been bent and twisted into a weird metal sculpture.

I still feel frozen. You'd have thought I'd be used to anything by now, but I can't stop staring at the scene in front of me: my Father thrashing back and forth, his jaw grinding, his fist shoved rhythmically from his side to his head and bloated eye. The crumpled metal blind on the dirty bare window makes a surrealistic backdrop to his agony.

Finally I go over to the driven form that is my Father. I am afraid to get too close, to get in the way of the frantic movements. "Daddy," I call out softly. "Daddy. It's me. Would you stop hurting yourself and come with me. We'll go out and get some lunch, Daddy. Please." But nothing. No response. No breaking of the trance state he is trapped in.

I cannot think of what to do. What to say. An ambulance, I think. I should call an ambulance. But what hospital do I take him to? What hospital takes Medi-Cal? Think, I tell myself. You have to think. His doctor. The unobtrusive man who was his doctor at the assisted living facility. Who didn't know what to do about his spitting. Or any of his other bizarre symptoms. But at least he was following his case. Checked his blood pressure once in a while. Got his toenails that were double in size with a thick yellow crust clipped at the facility. Gave him medication once for scabies.

Incredibly, the doctor is in his office. I can hear the near hysteria in my voice and the receptionist, alarmed, puts him on the phone. "See if you can get him in your car and take him to Sutter," he directs me. "Is there anyone that can help?" Yes, I realize, there are people who can help. "Get someone to help you with him. I'll call the hospital and let them know you're coming in. I'll meet you there in about an hour."

Direction. Purpose. Someone willing to help me advocate for my Father. Maybe I can make it through this grotesque dance after all.

Mary and I look at each other in confusion and horror. There is no way we can get him into the car between us. Not like this. I call Robert and he will leave work and arrive in twenty-five minutes. Thank god for small favors. My Father's rhythmic movement goes on, but by the time Robert arrives it has slowed down some.

Gradually, very gradually, my Father comes partly out of his trancelike state. His movements are more erratic now, less intense and less continuous. They lack the furiousness and the compulsive, driven rhythm. I am not as afraid to get close to him, partly because I am not alone.

Between the now semi-trancelike movements, we slowly lift him to an almost sitting position in the soaking, torn up bed. His clothing is as wet and crumpled as the sheets. One of us on each side, we shift and adjust his body to a leaning, almost standing position and we half-carry him toward the door, our arms and mouths filled with his breath and his sweat. We support my Father's almost folded form, broken like the mini-blinds, the gauze orange curtains, the soaking sheets and blanket, over to the waiting car and we lie him out on the back seat, a rigid, staring shell of a person, drained of his humanity.

And we drive him to the hospital, the frightening white place that has so often been his home.

THEY PUT MY Father on an IV at the hospital and the white
care and the habitual clenching and silence return. During the
next few days he stabilizes. His eye heals and only the old minor
jaw spasms and dripping of saliva remain. The hospital doesn't know
what to do with him, but they know that he needs to leave. Yes, they
are willing to keep him for the weekend. I consider taking him back
to Mary's. I have paid them for the damages, and they are willing to
try again. The doctor says he should go to a nursing home, but it is
up to me. I begin to relax. Decisions on where to put him. Easy stuff,
comparatively.

The next day when I enter his room I can feel the familiar sick-
ness. The intermediate calm has disappeared and my Father's body is
hooked up to tubes again and he is in the midst of a trancelike rigid
motion. His jaw is moving in large uncontrollable clenching movements, which are making him bite his lips raw. He has blood all over
his mouth, which the spasmodic grinding and biting has swollen to
several times its normal size. His eyes are hollow dark shadows of
pain in his unshaven face. No one is there with him. No one is doing
anything. Not even trying.

I run over to the desk to call a nurse. "Hasn't anyone seen my
Father?" I ask. "Where is the doctor?" The nurse is moderately apol-
ogetic. "Well, the doctor tried to get him to stop —we all have— but
nothing's helped."

I make the doctor come in—apparently it's gotten worse since
he was last there and he orders a combination of anti-anxiety and
anti-Parkinsonian medications through the IV that is feeding my
Father. The medications finally slow the movements down, but he is
still grinding and his mouth looks horrible and it is probable that he

will start taking apart his lips again when the meds wear off. "Do you think he could use a mouth appliance like the ones they give people who grind their teeth?" I ask the doctor.

"It could help, if you can find a dentist who would be willing to make one. I doubt Medi-Cal will pay for it."

"Maybe his dentist will come here," I say, and go to phone Dr. Light, whose careful work saving my Father's teeth can be seen in living action, doing quite a job on his mouth.

Dr. Light comes to the hospital the next morning to try to fit my Father for an appliance. "Are you sure you want this done?" he asks me carefully. "I doubt he'll be able to handle it by himself, and it will only be used here if the staff will put it on him."

"If there's any chance it'll help, let's get it done. Please. Whatever it costs." I say. And so Dr. Light makes a mold of my Father's pitiful teeth and the appliance is made on a rush by the next day. But the grinding subsides and doesn't get that bad again, and my Father doesn't end up using it after all. In a couple of days, his mouth, like his eye, begins to heal.

THE NEW PROBLEM is that my Father is unable or unwilling to eat or drink by himself and they can't keep him hooked up to an IV indefinitely. The gastroenterologist is sent in to talk to me. He explains that a gastronomy tube needs to be inserted through the skin and the abdomen to deliver food directly into my Father's stomach, so that he will not "waste away" when he can't or won't eat. "It's a fairly minor, routine operation in cases like this," he says. "And," he hesitates, "You don't have a choice. If you don't sign for your Father's operation, we'll get a court order to do it."

The surgery for the stomach tube is successful; the only problem is that my Father's lungs collapse after the surgery and when I arrive he is in intensive care inside a plastic tent with tubes going everywhere. At least his eyes are shut and I do not have to look into the vast blueness that does not respond. He looks like death and I think perhaps death would be merciful and for the best. To end this twisted, torturous game that is supposed to be his life. I look through the plastic again, at his distorted face, and feel overwhelming despair.

His doctor comes to see him later in the day. As if reading my thoughts he tells me my Father is looking pretty bad and there may not be much point keeping him alive. "It might be best to let him go," he says. "You're his only living relative and all you have to do is sign a form that refuses to use extraordinary measures to keep him alive."

I have already signed for the stomach tube. Now I am to sign for his death. "I'm sorry," I tell the doctor. "I can't. At least not yet."

And I was right, sort of. The next day his vital signs are closer to normal and he is back to moderate clenching, drooling, and silence.

No one knows what to do with my Father or what has caused any of the events that have happened or that follow. One doctor thinks he may have gotten dehydrated initially and that's what triggered the whole mess. Another says he has some symptoms of Parkinson's disease. But no one knows. I am exhausted, and I think it doesn't matter. The stomach tube means he can't go back to Mary's, even though he has started eating on his own. He has to be placed in a facility that has nursing staff so he can be fed and medicated through the tube if it becomes necessary again.

I have the weekend to think about placements. At least my Father is stable again. Unless the hospital calls with a new crisis, I am taking a sorely needed break.

I WALK THROUGH my front door, reeling from the insanity and despair I have been spending most of my waking hours trying to navigate—forget any attempt to influence.

In the family room, Chanti and two of her friends are working on a history/literature project that is due tomorrow. The oversized counter, that we designed using slats of thick pine, is almost covered with food, drinks, books, papers and pens; the murmuring tone is one of cooperation and concentration. Chanti at thirteen is able to listen deeply and empathically and with her unassuming, gentle presence and easy affection has become more and more desirable as a friend.

Through the glass doors to the backyard, beyond the orange tree and camellias, I see Kira, sixteen, who a teacher described as "the fulcrum that holds the group together," lying on the string double hammock with Brion, her steady boyfriend since junior high. Best friend Jolie and her boyfriend of the moment are hanging out on the grass laughing easily.

From the beginning, we were clear that we had our kids to enjoy them, not police them. We live close to the schools and our home is a magnet for the kids nearby, mostly because our only rules are don't intentionally hurt yourself or anyone else and try not to break anything. And when friends need a place to hang out and be themselves they can drop in at our home, no invitations or permissions necessary.

I try to breathe in the normalcy in the room, the smells, sounds, and colors of not-hospital, the troubles and struggles that are real but mostly temporary, problems that with care and gentleness can be negotiated and made better, even if not completely resolved.

I PREPARE MYSELF for another harrowing visit, as I walk down the hall to my Father's room, but I am completely unprepared for the meteoric shift from heartbreaking to breathtaking that is the new reality.

Three days ago my Father was "stable" which meant off the machinery and only doing the usual sporadic tongue and jaw spasms of tardive dyskinesia that he has lived with for years. He had begun drinking liquids, and while he wasn't eating much the stomach tube took care of that.

I anxiously enter the open doorway to my Father's room.

My Father is dressed in the clean light blue shirt and gray pants that I left for him, and he is sitting with his back toward me on the corner of the bed chatting with the nurse. I can hear the tail end of her voice and then I hear his voice, eager, clear and friendly, saying that the food here is about as good as at the Automat.

My Father turns toward me, sensing my presence, and, apparently delighted to see me, he says, "Hey, it's about time you got here. I've been waiting for hours. Let's blow this joint."

"Daddy," I say stupidly. "You're talking."

"I know," he replies. "Guess I shocked you, huh? Everyone else is in shock, too."

"It's amazing," says the nurse's aide. "One day he don't talk to no one, and the next he's the nicest man in the hospital."

"Aw, shucks," says my Father as they beam at each other in apparent camaraderie.

"We couldn't believe it. He woke up this way, asked for his clothes, dressed and shaved himself and said he was ready to go home."

"Well, I'm not sick, am I?" asks my Father.

It seems fairly obvious that he is just fine. I walk closer to the bed and give him a tentative hug. His arms reach out and he holds me close, pats my back. His arms that were a few days ago caught in the throes of rigid, trancelike movements, the arms that have not reached out in return since I had him flown to California, the arms that have not held me for almost twenty years, reach out and hold me close. I am stunned, in a state of shock. I have to talk to myself to be sure that this is not a fantasy or a dream.

"Well, what's new?" my Father asks me. "How's the kiddies? How's your life?"

I try to find out what he knows. He is aware of the date, the year—he's seen the newspaper— he knows Kira and Chanti's names and that he is in California. But he mostly knows the little things. How to make conversation, to joke around, how to be a warm and responsive human being.

One of the nurses comes by and says, "Hi Sam, how you doing pal?" and my Father waves cheerfully at her and introduces me. I recognize her as one of the nurses who was there when my Father was on tubes.

She shakes her head. "Unbelievable, isn't it?" She stops to talk to us. "Do you know what your Father said to me this morning when I told him he needed to get in the shower? He told me he was part cat and allergic to water. Then he said he'd only go in if I'd go in with him. I have to say with those pretty blue eyes it was a tempting offer," she teases him and he glows.

My mind is racing. I have to bring Robert and the kids here. They've never seen him intact. The video camera. I'll bring the camera. Maybe if my family sees him and it's on film I'll believe it's real. That he's real. Not a vegetable, not even a non-vegetable, but a warm, connected, fun-loving human being— the Father I grew up with, my daddy. No clenching, no agony, no silence.

My Father and I discuss the options from the meal menu. He prefers the Swiss steak to the ham and pineapple, cheesecake to ice cream. This is not a yes, no conversation. This is a normal conversation I could be having with anyone.

My Father doesn't want me to leave without him, but the nurses are firm. The doctor has seen him and said that he needs to stay for a day or two before he can go home. I tell him to relax and enjoy all the attention and that I'll be back with Robert and the kids in a few hours. As I start to leave, another nurse swings by and asks him if she can get him some filet mignon—he is the hero of the ward.

I go down the elevator with my heart pounding and tears filling my eyes.

ROBERT, KIRA, AND Chanti look at me as if I have gone insane or I am certainly exaggerating the changes that have taken place. Yet there is an excitement that I am generating that begins to be contagious. "Come on, you guys," I say. "I want you to see for yourself." I want to take the movie camera, but Kira, the authority on appropriateness at sixteen, says it will embarrass him, and I think yes the big videocamera could make him into a spectacle. And yet it seems like I can pull it off—pretend we're interviewing him or something. But I go along with Kira and leave it home. We go, the four of us, unencumbered by machinery.

They are stunned when they walk into the room. My Father is vital, alive, his skin tone has color for the first time since they've seen him. His wonderful silver-blue eyes are not vacant; they are alive with intelligence, humor, and presence. He gets up to meet them, puts his hand out to Robert and hugs and kisses Kira and Chanti. He jokes about the food, the nurses, and little things make him smile and even laugh. He is interested in what they are learning in school, teases them about boyfriends, wants to know all about them. I watch him for signs of mania, but I see no reason to worry. His eyes are not glazed and he sounds completely rational. I must be dreaming, I think, but no, whatever has seized his mind for years—all the years that I have wondered if his withdrawal was mental or physical— has released him. There seems to be no question that he has been in a state of some biochemical control that has kept the person he was from being able to be there or communicate. I think of all the times people have yelled at him, called him names, been certain that he was obstinate and "bad" and worse and I feel relief that the real person inside has not been those things: they have been the result of some physical aberration. But what was it, what kept him in a vegetable state for all these years? And what has jolted him out of it?

I try to see if my Father is completely back, and he passes every test. We take a walk down the hall and talk while Robert and the children go to get snacks at the cafeteria. I ask what he remembers about New York and if he recalls being gone for several years. He doesn't remember the lost years, so I can't find out from him what happened after he left the hospital so many years ago. "Was I in a hospital before then?" my Father asks. "What do you remember?" I ask him back, worried about what he should or shouldn't know. "I think it was a mental hospital," he says, looking at me for confirmation. I am caught off guard. We have never talked about his being in a mental hospital. It has always been a taboo subject, unless he was high, and then it was either a subject of derision or an ominous wall between us as

I tried to get him to sign himself in so I wouldn't have to. In between being high, we never spoke of what had happened and I don't know what to say. I am out of safe waters. I don't want to upset him and I don't know how I am supposed to respond. "You used to get depressed," I mumble vaguely, and sensing my discomfort my Father deftly changes the subject.

When we get back to his room, Robert and the kids are waiting. My Father sits down on the bed. Kira leans against the wall across from him and slides down until she is in a sitting position on a non-existent chair. Chanti copies her sister. "Comfortable?" my Father asks. "Mmhhmmm" Chanti says.

"It looks comfortable," I say, and I sit lightly on her lap. Robert follows me and balances on Kira. My Father looks amused at the sculpture before him, wrinkles his eyebrows as if trying to figure out what needs to be corrected in the scene, and then says to Robert, "Hey, Robert. You're too heavy for such a little kid. Hand me your glasses."

Before we leave I offer to give my Father my phone number so he can call if he wants to and he carefully writes down my name and number on his own. I think wryly that not that long ago he didn't even know we were related. He hasn't written anything readable in years.

I want to go but I don't want to go. As it gets later my Father helps me decide. On the back of an envelope he writes, "Go back to your home now or I will personally escort you out the door." He winks at me, and slowly the four of us leave the hospital, feeling exhausted and exhilarated.

M Y FATHER'S DOCTOR doesn't want to release him the next morning, not until his medical condition and his now anachronistic stomach tube have been re-examined and re-evaluated. And I am faced with so many things that have been neglected over the past weeks that I don't call my Father until the afternoon. I want to go back and see him, but I am also overwhelmed and I realize that when he comes home with me the next morning—assuming all is okay—there will be so much more to be done. My Father is happy to hear from me but is doing fine entertaining the hospital staff.

"Hey, you're tired, you're busy," my Father says, picking up on my ambivalence. "Why don't you take a break tonight and enjoy your kids. I'm not going anywhere—they won't let me out until morning—just don't forget to pick me up. I'll be ready for you, bright and early."

I realize that I have no plans for what to do with my Father now that he is normal. I need to find him a place to live—but not the kind of places I've been looking at. He won't need his feeding tube: he is eating like a champ, so no need of a nursing home. I know there are senior residences and furnished rooming houses in my area that could work. There are restaurants and stores nearby, a park to walk in. Maybe my Father can even get some part-time work, like I'd imagined many years ago, before he'd arrived in his vacant state. Maybe part of my fantasies can come true. Maybe Kira, who had thought a granddaddy was more special than a dolphin at Marine World over ten years ago could finally have a real grandfather: one who could respond and participate in our family.

I feel almost high. I have my Father back after twenty years! Just as good as new! And I am finally vindicated in my belief in my

Father's essential goodness and humanity, although I, too, have had periods of suspecting that my Father was uncaring and obstinate, and not brain-dead. What has happened is real. Underneath the layer of indifference and deadness, my Father is real.

I can't wait until the morning to take him home.

I FEEL A nervousness I cannot shake as I arrive at the hospital at 9:00 a.m. I pass it off as the usual trepidation. Of course I feel anxious. At various times my Father has been militant, hyperactive, depressed and not wanting to live, passed out from shock treatments, almost normal, and a vegetable. Visits to the hospital were always frightening: the unknown, a few floors or doors away.

But it isn't just an old, irrational fear with ties to the past. It belongs to the present.

When I go to his room my Father is not sitting up and waiting for me, dressed, with a twinkle in his eyes. He is not happily making conversation with the nurses. My Father is instead lying on his back, asleep, his jaw moving as it has done for so many years, in spasms that he is unable to control. I am not sure that he is back to his deathlike state, at first. I go over to his bed. "Daddy," I say, shaking him gently. "Daddy, it's me. Wake up." My Father opens his eyes and looks at me. I stare into the enormous, deep, silver-blue emptiness I have become accustomed to over the years since he has been in California. The light is gone out of his eyes. My Father stares back at me for a few seconds, closes his eyes again and turns over on his side, away from me. I feel my stomach knot over again, the nausea begin.

I leave the room and go out into the hall, holding my hand to my mouth to keep the scream from coming out of my throat. I go to the desk and the nurse looks at me in pity. "We don't understand it. He apparently didn't look very well late last night, and this morning he was—well, like he is now. I'm really sorry. He seemed like a nice man."

I cannot contain myself. She seems so caring. I begin to sob and I can't stop. Why hadn't I come yesterday? Maybe if I had come yesterday I could have done something. And yet I know that this, like everything about my Father, is out of my control. This bizarre thing that has entered my Father's body has a mind of its own and nothing I do or don't do makes any difference.

But if I had known that it would last for so short a time I could have come and talked to him, found out so much more about the empty places, the lost moments. I would have brought the video-camera, something, some way to make him solid, visible, concrete. Some way to keep even a small piece of my Father alive.

PART FIVE

DONE

I Am Spirit In The Wind

I TRY TO see my Father often enough so that the shame does not burn me. If I do not see my Father, he joins the ranks of the loved/ known/cared for by no one. There is no one else but me. Even if he never speaks to me or asks how I am or what I feel. Even if his eyes in their silver-blue vastness never quite meet mine. I am mixed in my mind between feeling a certain possessive satisfaction over the uniqueness of my role and a stronger overriding rancor at the people who have abandoned him or pushed him down into this grim world of the almost dead. And resentment, because it is a burden I do not want, in my life that is finally filled with kinder, gentler moments and rimmed with hope.

The conditions at this, the end of my Father's descent to nursing home politely labeled convalescent hospital, are not as bad as they could be. He doesn't exactly belong in a nursing home because he is not sick, and he is mobile—no cane, walker or wheelchair necessary. There is flowered wallpaper in the halls and the staff is friendly enough and if you can get by the stench and the people groaning in wheelchairs pleading in contorted positions for a crumb of attention, without drowning in the depth of their unanswerable needs, you can have a civil conversation with the nurses or the orderlies, most of the time. As I walk by the other residents toward my Father I sicken myself by involuntarily relating this time to many years before choosing a small black and white puppy with freckles over so many others at the pound who barked at me with their eyes moist, running back and forth from the chicken wire fence to the wall, wagging their tails low, cocking their heads in desperation or lying in corners with blank stares; and the cats and kittens with their emery-board tongues scraping burning maps of guilt on my wrist and fingers. Then it was a refrain that kept going over and over in my mind: every one you do not take you are condemning to death.

There are not enough people to care for all the lost animals, the lost souls, the lost bodies. What good is recognizing how little my share amounts to compared to the thick whirlpool of pain around me? What is to be done? At least I can see my Father twice a month, and pretend I am doing something for someone.

IT'S TIME TO leave the warmth and safety of my home to take my Father out to lunch. Even though there have been few incidents over the past several months, the last thing I want to do is drive to the depressing nursing home and go through the every other week motions of being a good daughter. Robert, Kira, Chanti and I are in the middle of a conversation about ways we can get more involved in the struggle for world peace. The international musical play, *Peace Child,* performed in Sacramento, with Kira in a minor role, has inspired us. Robert has been a peace activist for as long as I've known him, and the play, with a mission of creating hope and global peace, has given us direction and purpose. It is an inspiring show for Kira and Chanti and many other children, as the entire cast is comprised of young people under eighteen. Its central story is of two children of diplomats from Russia and the United States who befriend each other and, through the power of drama and song, convince the adults, Mr. President and Mr. Secretary, to listen to each other and find common ground to peace; and to end the Cold War that could blow up the world in a fireball, destroying the future for everyone. Kira and Chanti participate in the local children's choir that forms to carry the message of the play to schools, churches, a shopping mall and even the California State Fair. I can hear in my mind, as I drive away, the words to one of the songs: "I have a vision, I have a dream."

And while my family continues to consider global challenges and how they can best help make world peace possible, I arrive at the nursing home to find my Father in his room dressed in a hideous, dark green-yellow fifties suit two sizes too large that makes his eyes look like brown mud, his skin jaundiced. And instead of world issues

I become riveted on my Father's appearance; my mission, my intention, my vision and dream becomes simply to improve the color and fit of my Father's clothing.

I have again bought my Father almost two hundred dollars worth of blue shirts, navy and gray pants, underwear and socks, and the staff has this month again managed to lose it all. Too many people, too many beds. I look my Father over and only then notice that he has no socks on under his unlaced shoes. I cannot find any socks in the room. I am upset, but mostly just acting upset, inside blaming myself because I could have put up a sign, like one of the other resident's family has, on the two feet of space that passes for a closet, that says: *Do Not Wash Clothes. Family Will Take Care Of It.*

I tell my Father to wait in his room until I return and I am directed to the woman in charge of patient services. She has this all down to a science or an art. She doesn't even say if you've got a problem about his clothing maybe you should wash them yourself. She is sorry but there's new staff and they can't seem to keep it straight whose stuff is whose. "So all the time spent shopping and marking my Father's name on collars and waistbands and sideways on socks is wasted?" I ask her.

"Well, maybe we can find some of them," she responds optimistically. "Let's look."

We go first to the mess in the laundry area. A worker looks at me suspiciously and continues throwing underwear and socks from bin to bin, hanging wrinkled shirts and pants on bent wire hangers. "Do you recognize anything?" the patient services woman asks me. The heat is overwhelming and the constant motion of the machines and the woman throwing things and moving things are dizzying. The clothing is jammed together so tightly it's hard to distinguish individual pieces. We go over a small area, pulling and pushing at clothing as if we are at a bargain rack in a department store. No luck. Trying to find his socks in the bins doesn't net any of his gray socks either. We compromise and borrow some with the name Jim barely readable on the sole.

"Let's go look in the other closets," she says to me, undeterred. "Maybe his clothes are in someone else's room." This starts to feel kind of like fun, almost like a scavenger hunt, definitely easier than looking at the sad, broken faces and bodies in the halls. Or talking nervously to the blank stare that is my Father. We walk authoritatively into the other rooms. Only one man complains, telling us to leave his things alone. "Well, now, don't you worry about that one bit, honey," she tells him, as she pores through his worn, faded clothing. "We're not gonna take nothing that belongs to you." She is bright and cheerful with the residents, especially those who are able to speak a few words, although the words do not always correspond to the context of the conversation. Most of the people seem not to care if she talks to them or not, but she doesn't seem put off. Good boundaries, I decide. And she seems kind enough. Steady and kind. I guess it's a job to her, and she makes the best of it.

After several failures, we eventually find two of my Father's blue shirts and a pair of his gray pants squashed in between other clothing in someone else's room. I pull them out, thank the patient services woman and return to my Father's room where he is standing, waiting. I begin the tedious process of getting my Father to change. Again. I tell him nonchalantly as I can that he needs to change his clothes so we can go out for lunch. But he shakes his head and turns away. He will not be sold on changing his clothes again. He has changed. He seems to know that much. Or he's picked up my uncertainty. He certainly doesn't care how bizarre he looks. Even in his most sane, glorious days he didn't care about appearances. All that work finding his clothing for nothing. And yet I secretly add the scavenger hunt to the credits I give myself for time spent seeing my Father.

"I won't take you out Daddy unless you at least put socks on," I say, taking a chance that I can get one small concession from him.

He looks down at his feet. "You're not wearing any socks, Daddy," I say. "It's cold out." My Father looks confused. "Sit down here on your bed and put these on. Okay? Please." I say gently. He takes the socks labeled Jim from my outstretched hand, collapses on the thin mattress and slowly lifts one foot from his shoe.

I wonder as I wait for him what it must be like to be in a nursing home. Perhaps I would be a resident someday. I wonder if it is worse to observe it, an outsider looking in, than it is to be there. Is the imagined horror worse than the reality. Is watching someone's pain as bad as experiencing it or sometimes even worse?

My Father has put his socks on by himself and his shoes. His head is hanging over his dark green-yellow covered thighs. "Okay, Daddy. Guess we can go to lunch now. I'm starving. How about you?"

He rises to his feet, clasps his hands behind his back, slightly bent, and follows me past the people in wheelchairs staring at us and grunting as we go out the glass doors into the fresh, cool scent of the world outside.

A friend comments that nursing homes affect everyone, that there is hardly anyone who doesn't know someone who is in one and that everyone would relate to these feelings about being there. Finally I am in the stream of normality, visiting my aged father in a nursing home. Finally, we belong.

I HAVE GIVEN up on communicating with my Father, and he clearly doesn't care one way or the other, so there's nothing more I can do. Mother is another story.

Living around the corner has been basically good, and the only ongoing issue has been that she comes into our house uninvited and without calling or knocking and we have bitter talks about boundaries for which she never forgives me. Mother has never learned to drive so Robert or I are her drivers when she needs to go places not in walking distance. For larger shopping trips, I take her to Raley's and sometimes it goes okay. This one day it is not okay. I am tired and do not want to wait while she examines every lettuce in the bin to see which is the best and largest and I am dangerously rude. I honestly don't remember the words, but I know I said things I regretted later. We have already had too many confrontations. Mother talks nonstop, and I do not have the patience to listen, simulate interest or tune out and think my own thoughts. We have had innumerable discussions about this. When I take her to shop for clothing I stipulate that I have to have silence for ten-minute intervals each hour or two that we're together, which always ends up being awkward and uncomfortable.

So after this one day that I am unjustifiably rude and sarcastic, I take Mother back to her home and bring in her packages for once in unasked for silence.

And Mother seems to have decided to keep the silence. She doesn't call me all week and I leave it at that.

When the mail comes the next week with a letter from Mother I do a double take but am not prepared at all for its contents. The letter lets me know how terrible I have been to her since I was eight years old. She believes this is because I have been punishing her for the mistakes she made when I was smaller. I am self-centered and rude when she has done nothing to deserve it. She should, she writes, have been stricter with me, not let me get away with things. She is through with me making her feel guilty and never showing her affection (she is right about this last part) and wants me to apologize.

I find myself shaking, but not in shock until I read the signature:

"With unconditional love,
Your mother"

WHAT TO DO? This time the question is not with my Father, but with Mother. I have been a family therapist for almost twenty years and what I have seen in my practice is that when adult children try to talk to their parents about their past and how their childhood has affected their present, their sense of self, and their relationships they usually receive negative reactions from their parents, no matter how gently they broach the subject.

I try my best to put myself in Mother's place and when I do I realize that there are no instructions for her and other parents on how to respond appropriately to their grown children's attempts to communicate about the past. They believe they are being attacked, and so they attack, distract or retreat in response.

And so, with this focus, in just three weeks I write a query, first chapter, and chapter outline for a book for parents, which I give the working title, *Making Peace With Your Adult Children.* The query letter that I send to several publishing houses begins with the sentence: "Everyone wants to be a good parent, but even more everyone wants to have been a good parent."

Two amazing things happen. Eighteen publishing houses want a full proposal from me, a never before published writer; and when I call Mother to tell her I started writing a book to help us reconnect and that I have several pages I'd like to share if she wants to read them, she says, yes, she does.

I work on a proposal, send it out, and get three offers for the book. I choose Plenum, and work with Linda Greenspan Regan, a brilliant editor who helps me clarify my vision and further soften my approach. Under her guidance, an outline for a 150 page book becomes 375 pages hardback, and helps Mother and me, as we go through the exercises together, work through some of our differences.

In the acknowledgements I write:

My original motivation for writing this book was to explain to my mother, Lea (Lillian) Bargad, what I needed from her. She has been willing and eager to know what this is and to work on repairing our relationship. I thank her for her stability, strength, and endurance.

I give Mother a copy and she beams with pride.

I also write: I want to thank my dad, Samuel Levy, for his gentleness, humor, and his ability to see things in unique and special ways, which have been the foundation of my creativity.

I show my Father the front cover of the book with my name on it, which he looks at without comprehension. Then I read the acknowledgement to him, and receive the glimpse of a smile that could mean anything and probably nothing.

My book sells fairly well. Janet Goldstein at HarperCollins buys the paperback rights from Plenum and more copies make it into the bookstores. I find myself speaking at various places; I even give one keynote speech to 300 people that terrifies me before, during and after.

So I am now a published author, but the tiny, suppressed part of me that thought it might help me reach my Father was wrong, and while it helps Mother and me repair our past, it doesn't help with our present; Mother remains demanding and difficult to relate to and I remain intolerant, demanding and difficult myself.

Throughout this time, Kira and Chanti seem to be dealing with the challenges that plague all teenagers with relative ease and aplomb, with little of the desperation I felt during those years. They have always had the freedom to make their own decisions, and without control issues to deal with we rarely argue. Kira has chosen to go to UC Santa Cruz in the fall to study theater. Chanti will enter her sophomore year of high school and further develop her own sense of self and leadership style without her sister in the limelight.

I watch them in awe and admiration, and hope in my deepest heart and soul that our connection will continue through adulthood, and that I will not pass the legacy of unhappiness and resentment on to my beloved children.

I HAVE TWO chances in the next few months to see how much progress I have made in my ongoing struggle to come to terms with my inability to reach my Father and Mother and to test my parenting skills. The first challenge comes while helping Chanti at her high school.

"They've cut all the counselors," Chanti tells me, shocked and angry, as she walks into the family room after school. "All of them! It's not like we had enough to begin with!" Chanti has watched us teach parenting classes in our home—sometimes even called in as a volunteer when someone needed a child to practice on; has participated in our emotional family meetings, where we listened and (usually) resolved conflicts; and was one of the students chosen and trained by the counselor in middle school to assist peers with problems, so she is a strong advocate of counseling.

Several days later, I find out that Chanti has taken matters into her own hands and has received permission to start a pilot peer counseling program at McClatchy High School. "You'll help me get it off the ground, right?" she asks, and three other licensed therapists are soon enlisted to bring peer counseling, including family therapy exercises, listening, sharing, and problem solving skills to the school.

At the first meeting, a family therapist friend and I join in the circle of twelve students who have signed up. Chanti begins, sharing about herself first and then asking the students to share who they are, what they need and what they hope to contribute. She intuitively and gently supports and moves from one person to the next, while keeping us all engaged, in depth and in balance. It would seem to an observer looking in that there is no facilitator and we, the professionals, are unnecessary.

Another therapist and I set up a form of psychodrama to help the peer counselors understand their family patterns so that when they work with their peers they will be less likely to transfer their issues onto them and also to experience making healthy decisions about the kind of families they will eventually create.

One of the students directs four others in a construct of her family: the father, mother, sister and herself. In the dramatization, her mother is at the stove behind the closed front door, and her younger sister and she, age five and seven, stand outside in their coats and scarves, their suitcases ready at their sides. They are waiting for their father to pick them up. The scene freezes. We all wait. And wait. And wait. Tears begin.

"How long did you have to wait?" I ask, gently.

"Sometimes," she whispers, "he didn't show up at all."

"How would you have liked it to be?"

She walks over to the students playing her family and brings her father who is off-stage up to the doorway. She has him embrace the two children gently, then take their valises and lead them off the stage.

"What did you learn that you can take into your future?" we ask her.

"I will never let myself or my children be harmed like that. I will find someone I can depend on to keep his word."

I stay in my professional, supportive role, but even after all this time it is hard not to go back to being a child myself, waiting nervously for my Father, showing up in so many disguises, if he showed up at all.

Kira, meantime, enchanted with theater and women's studies, is looking forward to her first year of college at UC Santa Cruz. Leaving Brion, though, who is staying in Sacramento for college, is clearly traumatic—they have been together almost five years, as long as many marriages. My first child leaving home feels horrible, even though we have always said that you have to give your children wings as well as roots. At least, I comfort myself, she has decided to enroll in a college on the West Coast.

I start feeling jealous of all the attention Brion is getting. Kira barely talks to us for weeks, except about how much she will miss Brion. We finally load her, miserable about leaving Brion behind, into the car to take her to her new school.

I cannot help myself. As we help Kira unpack her clothing and other belongings in the small closet of her dorm room, I say, using no skills whatsoever: "Well, the least you could do is pretend you're going to miss us."

"What are you talking about?" Kira wants to know, appalled by my statement.

"Brion, Brion, Brion. I'm sorry, but couldn't you save just a little bit of misery for missing your parents?"

"What?" Kira repeats. "Of course I'll miss you guys! But I know I'm going to see you again, and again and again. You're part of who I am. I don't know what will happen between me and Brion when we're apart. That's why I'm so sad and scared to leave him."

And it all kicks in. Unless some unforeseen illness or accident happens, Kira won't have to miss Robert and me like I had to miss my Father, so often and unexpectedly, and yes, even Mother, with her moods and need to be in control. I suddenly remember a terrible card I gave Mother when I was about eight years old for Mother's Day. My grandfather had let me pick out the card and it said: *To my mother, always here when I needed you here.* I had added the letter *T* in large print before the first *here* to change it to *There* so it read, *To my mother, always There when I needed you here.* Now it seems incredibly cruel, but it was a plea for help, for her to be here, present, open to my needs as well as her own, when I needed her.

"I'm sorry, Kira," I say, embarrassed by my regression into my child-hood, instead of being present with hers. "That makes perfect sense."

And so we leave to go back to our home, and I am resigned to missing my daughter on her terms, happily surprised when the next day I get a sweet phone call from Kira, telling me about her roommate, her orientation to classes, the ocean at sunset, and that yes she misses me and loves me and is so grateful that I am her mom.

FOR A FEW years, this nursing home has worked reasonably well for my Father and me. There haven't been any outrageous or threatening events or out-of-control episodes that couldn't be handled.

As long as my Father is in the central part of the nursing home, he can get out of his room and be around people—the staff, visitors—and he is only a few steps from the small library. Sometimes I find him there standing by a table reading or looking through magazines, looking disheveled, worn out, but intact enough to get by. Rosa, the staff member who most often takes care of my Father, tells me he is a nice man. Today, holding a tray of leftover food she is about to bring to the kitchen, she says when she sees me walk in, "He is right there, at the end of the hall, see, in the chair waiting for you."

Sometimes my Father half-smiles when I get near. He lifts himself unsteadily from the chair and follows me to the car for our usual drive to the Sizzler, where he loads his plate with spaghetti and meatballs from the buffet table. Throughout the meal he struggles to control the erratic motion of his tongue and the involuntary clenching of his jaw when he tries to swallow, which have gotten progressively worse over the years. So toxic, medications with their horrific side effects.

It is always humiliating to take my Father out in public, even though he is dressed well enough in his light blue shirt and navy blue pants. People look at him and I am fiercely protective. *What are you staring at?* I want to say and don't. And sometimes I see him through their eyes as pieces of spaghetti fall out of his mouth back onto the plate or on the table, his jaw making jerking motions, silver-blue eyes watering.

But these are the good times. Before the new supervisor is hired at the nursing home and decides that a walking zombie perennially in the front hall area is a turnoff to visitors and moves my Father into a back section—more like the back ward at Brooklyn State Hospital. And my Father is no longer under the care of Rosa, the sweet woman who seemed to genuinely care about him.

IT DOESN'T SOUND like a big change, but it was. There were over a hundred patients there and, the way the nursing home was laid out, to get to my Father's new room you had to go to the end of the main hall where he used to be, then turn right and walk to the end of that long hall and then go right again, to the farthest, most remote end of the building, where you would be isolated and unable to figure out how to get to the main areas, if you were disoriented to begin with.

So when I went to pick up my Father, he would no longer be sitting waiting or reading a magazine. He would be lying in bed in his room staring at nothing. And his cleanliness deteriorated, and his clothing didn't get changed. And no one seemed to be responsible and certainly no one cared. I finally got to discuss it with the new director, a tall, heavyset go-getter of a man, who knew how to be polite but firm, a toxic combination.

Then something happened to my Father's throat, and I couldn't figure out what it was. It seemed to stick more than before and swallowing was more difficult. When we went out he ate less and he could barely swallow his root beer or even water.

More people stared. He had a bad odor. We sat closer to the corner.

It was a long wait in-between the every-other-week chore of seeing him that I had set for myself. The worse he got, the less I wanted to go.

The next time I took him out to lunch he ate almost nothing, drank a few drops and choked. I brought him back early and talked to the staff person at the desk. "Is he eating and drinking?" I asked her and she called someone from the back. I waited and waited and finally was assured that he was fine. He'd been eating and drinking fine.

I was certain this was a lie. But everyone was polite and firm and I did not have it in me to argue with polite and firm.

I called the next day to be told again, "Yes, he is fine."

I SHOULD GO BACK and check. I know this as well as I know anything on earth and yet I do not go. And the weekend I am scheduled to go, I do not go. I wait three weeks before I can bring myself to get in the car and drive to the nursing home, terrified of what I will find.

I pass the front desk, say hi to one of the polite, firm women, walk down the long hall, turn to the right, go down that long hall, turn right again to the last door where my Father now lives. I knock on the door to let him know that I am here and call, "Hi Daddy—it's me. I'm here to take you to the Sizzler." And then I see him lying on the bed. He has lost all his weight; he looks like a corpse with only his eyes recognizable. His jaw is moving but no one has shaved him or helped him out of bed, I suspect for days. "*Daddy, oh my god, Daddy,*" I cry and touch him gently, "*I'm so sorry, so so sorry.*"

And now I am in action form. "*I'll be right back,*" I say and I am in no mood to be trifled with. The long walk down the hall, left down the next hall and left again to the front desk where I demand an ambulance be called, now, not another second to wait. "You call 911 and get them to pick up my Father this second," I scream. "He is dying from dehydration and not one person here noticed? What is wrong with you? Call 911 right now."

And when the paramedics arrive I watch them lift a piece of his skin on his arm that gives no resistance: it is dried paper. They roll his dried skin and bones from his bed to the stretcher, while his eyes watch and his jaw does its ugly dance. I am assured that they will immediately start him on fluids in the ambulance. The long drive following in my car to Mercy Hospital, the short wait till he is admitted: no one wants him seen. I sit in the waiting room, numb, for an hour or two until I am told kindly to go home and rest; he is asleep on his drip and there is nothing I can do.

WHEN I RETURN to the intensive care unit the next morning I'm stunned to see that in less than twenty-four hours my Father has been pumped up almost back to his old shape, like a balloon that lost its air and has had it blown back in. His cheeks are not hollow anymore and the skin on his arms is puffed up like a normal person's arms.

I move closer to the bed to say something but my Father is swimming in strange waters that don't include me. He has oxygen tubes up his nose and he is hooked to a drip, and sleeps in an unworld that I have yet to inhabit.

For several more days he stays in the hospital being monitored. On the fifth day, he is finally awake and seems to recognize me, but he is still having trouble swallowing and is unable to eat solid food.

Then comes the question: "Do you want us to reopen his stomach tube?" There's a question about whether it is even possible after five years, and it would likely entail new surgery to reopen the area. Another surgery, they say, is not an easy procedure to endure. But there is no reason to think he will be able to eat by himself again, and he can't stay indefinitely in the hospital. What do I want them to do?

What to do with my Father. What do I do with my Father?

A ND THE ANSWER is given to me the next morning at 4 a.m. when the phone rings and I pick it up to hear a woman's voice inform me that if I want to see my Father alive again I need to get to the hospital right now. His heart is giving way.

But by 4:30 a.m., when I arrive at the hospital, the emergency is over. A machine is breathing for my Father, and he is stable once again. The nurse apologies for waking me when my Father is clearly not yet dead.

I hang around the hospital for an hour, then return home to not think.

That afternoon I come back to sit with my Father and, after a half-hour of watching and listening to him lying there being breathed into, something seems slower, somehow less intense, an almost ease that hasn't been there. I want so much to touch my Father, but I can't. I want to say something supportive and loving, but I have no voice. And then I hear the real change. And I realize that the machine is breathing into him but he is no longer there.

The nurse is checking the patient in the next bed, and I get up and tap her lightly on her shoulder. "I think my Father is gone," I whisper. She follows me and sees him not breathing. "Do you want me to have him resuscitated?" she asks me and I stare at her in disbelief and horror. "Please, leave him alone," I beg. "Leave my Father alone, to go in peace."

I watch them unhook the machines and I see the slight bit of color left in my Father's face and hands drain out. I have no idea how to feel.

And as I drive out of the hospital parking lot I hear, almost as my Father's actual voice, "I'm free. Finally, I'm free."

I drive slowly back home, empty and overwhelmed and shivering, to find Chanti, nineteen, coming out of her car onto the street at the same time as I arrive. She takes one look at me and walks quickly over and draws me into her arms, and holds me close to her, so I can let go and sob, with no barriers, questions or answers; and after, when we go into our house and we talk of other things, she continues to hold me lovingly in the boundless compassion of her green-brown eyes.

JUST A FEW of us so much of the time. I wonder as always what it must be like to be part of a big family. And now there is one less. There is no one to attend my Father's burial except us, the immediate family as we are called. I hire a rabbi who I do not know to do a facsimile of a traditional Hebrew service in the warm April air. Mother has foresightedly paid not just for one but for two plots at the Jewish cemetery a few miles away. "I figured I might as well get one for your father, too," she told me a few years back when she realized her move to California was permanent. She has also put money towards caskets. I quickly pass the mahogany and other extravagant coffins and pick out a plain coffin constructed with wooden nails—raw, unfinished, sanded, carved wood; not a box—a chest, with a wooden Jewish star of David carved on top with soft edges.

We walk along the grass dotted with gravestones until we find the gravediggers who have finished the burial hole and see the casket with my Father inside set to one side. The rabbi arrives in a few minutes. He is a short, heavy man dressed in a suit that is too small. He is disdainful and appalled when he sees that we don't have the minimum ten men present, as required by Jewish law, to make up a "minyan" for the service.

Nevertheless, he reads a prayer, a brochah from the Torah that is vaguely familiar to only Mother and me. He reads it too quickly; let's get this over with.

But we make him wait for our small ceremony to finish before allowing him to signal the men from the funeral home that it's time to lower my Father into the ground. "We have some things to say first," I tell him coldly.

I distribute small, deep turquoise cards with a peace bird over the world on the front cover. Inside is the poem by Mary Elizabeth Frye:

Do not stand at my grave and weep
I am not there. I do not sleep.
I am a thousand winds that blow.
I am the diamond glints on snow.
I am the sunlight on ripened grain.
I am the gentle autumn rain.

When you awaken in the morning's hush
I am the swift uplifting rush
Of quiet birds in circled flight.
I am the soft stars that shine at night.
Do not stand at my grave and cry;
I am not there. I did not die.

A separate paper, folded in half, outlines our program.

On the cover I have printed "In Memory of Samuel Levy," with the words to "Let Me Call You Sweetheart" underneath. Inside are the lyrics for "Side By Side" and "Let There Be Peace On Earth." The back has my Father's quote, "What's your rush . . . you going to a funeral?"

I talk about how important my Father was to me, how gentle, kind and funny; his connection to my travels in mystery, beauty and divergence; the reminder that often the measurable is meaningless.

I quote my Father: "Love is a must, far, far more important than the Yankee dollar that cannot kiss one back."

Robert reads the letter he has composed:

To Sam:

Thinking about you and the better times we had and didn't always have. You are on our shoulders, on our mind. Remember Brooklyn, that last exit, playing, shopping with Danny, Canarsie, Nathan's, lots of sauerkraut and mustard. We splurged at Bloomingdales, new pants for a tired Sam. Then flight to somewhere, meet and assist Sacramento. Find a home, Poverty Hill, South of

Broadway Gardenia House, Kathy's kind care after Brooklyn last exits.

Precious meeting with Kira and Chanti by the river throwing balls in a natural communion. Shirts and chocolates at Christmas brought sad smiles to your hoping, soft face.

As years passed, you and time passed by us. Nursing home and beyond felt like the end of the long road. After neglect, you like Kafka's *Hunger Artist* wouldn't eat, nothing gained, nothing lost. End game.

Your last supper, a plastic choker in your throat reminding us we are all just living ahead of that last choker, the ancient death rattle we all will hear. So now you are memory, brittle love.

Letters from a happy camp. Speak memory. Let It Be. Let It Be. See you on the endless karma wheel in the Coney Island of our minds. See you in all familiar places!

Bob

We sing "Let Me Call You Sweetheart" and "Side by Side" and end with "Let There Be Peace on Earth."

The Rabbi finally gets to nod to the men and they lower the casket into the ground. Robert has brought fresh fragrant roses—yellow, pink, multicolor orange and yellow and bright red for this occasion and after we do the requisite traditional flinging of one shovel of dirt each down into the grave I toss a yellow rose into the dirt covering my Father's coffin to the Rabbi's horror and we hold hands and sing "The Yellow Rose of Texas," one of the songs my Father used to croon in harmony with his brothers, Herbie and Joe.

When we are finished, just before the gravediggers fill the rest of the grave with dirt, the Rabbi sings in his raspy, harsh tone: "Yisgadal yiskadash shmay raba," and quickly leaves the gravesite.

And after a while, we return home, no longer encumbered by my Father's pain.

THE DANCE COMPANY Kira is in has received a teaching and performance contract in Portland for the summer, and I have signed up for a women's retreat in Waldport on the Oregon Coast. We will drive together and when our paths divide, my daughter will take the car to Portland and I will meet up with a carpool going along the Oregon Coast.

My Father has been gone for only two months and we talk about him on the road. I tell Kira it would have been fitting if he had died a day earlier, on April first, as April Fool's Day would have been his day of choice to die if he had been his old self. Having seen him in his normal state during the brief time he came back a few years ago, she believed me.

Kira hates sitting in the car and every time we come to a beach she pleads to get out and run and dance along the shore, tossing her shoes and socks off on the sand with abandon. And on this wide, solitary beach in the early afternoon we run together, Kira racing ahead and returning to find me, playing among kelp and sea shells, and suddenly I almost hear my Father's voice, channeling his easy and idiosyncratic wordplay. Kelp echoes into help and then don't tell, the shell fell down the well, and when we find dried fish bones the words turn to wishbones and there they are in front of me, pictures of my Father and Mother on Thanksgiving, the backdrop of ivy vines laddering up white bricks on washable wallpaper in our tiny kitchen. Mother, the civilized one, is in the process of tearing the entire turkey skeleton, mostly devoid of anything but bones, in half, with all her might, and there is my Father watching her and egging her on, making her laugh and cry at the same time. Here he is with a tissue in his hand patting at her tears, smiling at the camera, until the turkey's frame is unceremoniously and unevenly snapped apart, and sometimes, sometimes there is the salvaging of the wishbone and Mother lets me and my Father hold the ends, each trying to get closer to the center for advantage, and we pull up until one of us gets the big side with the top edge and with it the granting of a wish, a wish for a moment or a day or even a week of peace, a wish that would sometimes even come true.

The theme of the retreat is completing the past and at Djohariah's home ten of us are given clay to mold into whatever we want to represent completion. I sculpt a relief of a young woman's profile in white clay holding a rose that I sculpt from red-brown clay. I use slip to connect them and to place the girl and rose in the center of an oval red brown base I have constructed. The piece evolves as I go. When I finish I see that I am the woman and the flower is an offering to my Father, a way to leave him a gift so I can let go of the rest.

Our next instruction is to set up altars in remembrance of those we have lost. I have brought a copy of the deep turquoise half-sheet from the funeral service and I place it like a card on the altar with the candle that has been offered to each of us behind it. In front I place the piece I have made from clay.

We all light our candles and start to move toward the center of the room, when suddenly there is a flame and something has caught fire. The person nearby quickly smothers it with her breath and her hands and I see it is my Father's card that has burned . . . but how it has burned!

The words that remain clear after the fire are . . .

I am

I am

And, from nowhere I understand, come the words that I will later write on my Father's headstone: *I Am Spirit In The Wind.*

To further complicate the mystery that was and perhaps is my Father, to the side of the sculpture I see an almost perfectly shaped heart, formed from part of the card's black ash; and I am torn between a rational perspective of random events and an uneasy respect and reverence for the fugitive unknown.

ACKNOWLEDGEMENTS

I WANT TO thank those in this profession who have helped keep me out of mental wards and on the safe side of the couch. I owe my sanity in part to my therapist, David Fay. Besides my family—my daughters Kira and Chanti, who taught me more about love than I could ever teach them—I am held in the arms of Thomas Szasz, RD Laing, Fritz Perls, Carl Rogers, Thomas Gordon, Joanna Macy, Virginia Satir, and Peter Breggin. Their work is predicated on the power of empathy; before you or your loved ones follow the medical model, please read and carefully consider their work.

Literary artists and brave warriors, Joanne Greenberg, *I Never Promised You A Rose Garden* and Ken Kesey, *One Flew Over The Cuckoo's Nest*, whose McMurphy is a stunningly close rendition of my father in the manic state.

My father, whose words and struggle became my own, thank you. Thank you to my mother who believed in my ability with language, gave me strength and taught me persistence. And to Robert Claude Smith, artist and activist, for his love, friendship, and gentleness with my father.

I am indebted for editing and believing in my work to Gina Bliss, Lisa Bertaccini, and Mildred Ehrlich and to friends and readers Kathryn Gronke, Phoebe Celestin, Laurie Heller, Alexis Condy, Pauli Hakensen, Sharon Levinsky, Janet Greenwood, Rochelle Sherbert, and Bobbi Knapp. Thank you to Stefan Danielski for his generosity and sensitive, brilliant cover design and to Laurence Brauer for his patience and careful formatting.

Author Laura Davis has, as always, been a continuing support. Janet Goldstein, editor extraordinaire, convinced me to focus this book on my life as well as on my father's, and helped make *Missing Father* into a more accessible read. I am grateful to her also for the book title.

Thank you, my breathtaking children and grandchildren, and my husband, Ray Bacigalupi, who has shown up and loved me in a consistent way no one else ever has.

Shauna L. Smith, MSW has been a Licensed Marriage and Family Therapist in private practice for over thirty years. She is the author of *Making Peace With Your Adult Children: A Guide to Family Healing* (HarperCollins) and numerous articles, short stories and poems. She lives in Northern California with her husband.